CHINA · 7000 YEARS OF DISCOVERY

A special exhibition produced by the
China Science and Technology Museum
in cooperation with the
Ontario Science Centre, Toronto (May 1 to October 31, 1982)
Museum of Science and Industry, Chicago (June 1 to October 2, 1983)
Pacific Science Center, Seattle (March 1 to August 31, 1984)

WRITTEN AND EDITED BY:
China Science and Technology Palace Preparatory Committee
and the Ontario Science Centre
(Comparisons between East and West provided by the Ontario Science Centre)

CONSULTING WRITER: Richard Longley

ISBN 0-7743-6993-0

Design: Ontario Science Centre
Typesetting: Cooper & Beatty, Limited
          Mono Lino Typesetting Company
          Limited
Printed in Canada

Cover photo: Seismograph. See pages 30-31.
Title page: An incense clock used by
          astronomers.

Acknowledgements:

The publishers thank the following for
  their contributions to this book:
Yiu Ming Bau
Ian Buttars
Paula Chabanais Productions
Jerome Ch'en, York University, Toronto
Tom Clarke, McLaughlin Planetarium,
  Royal Ontario Museum, Toronto
East Asian Library, University of Toronto
Far Eastern Department, Royal Ontario
  Museum
Ursula Franklin, University of Toronto
Robert Garrison, University of Toronto
James Hsu, Royal Ontario Museum
Pamela Kanter
Mrs. C.Y. Lee
Paul Levine
Joseph Needham, Cambridge University
Bruce Pomeranz, University of Toronto
Patricia Proctor, Royal Ontario Museum
Flavia Redelmeier
Stephen Ripley
Hsio-yen Shih
Nathan Sivin, University of Pennsylvania
John E. Vollmer, Royal Ontario Museum
All institutions and individuals in China
who contributed to this book.

Photographs and illustrations courtesy of:
Cambridge University Library, Cambridge: centre 59; Champion International Corporation: 6; Richard Longley: top 25, top and bottom left/right 56, centre right and bottom: 62; Jack McMaster: top 9, top 11, top 14, 34, right and bottom left 35, top right 42, top 46, top 50; Royal Ontario Museum: top left 42, top right 44, top and centre left/right 45, left 47; Shangwu Publishing House, H.K.: top right 18; Shujing Tushuo ch. 32, p. 3A, China 1909: right 58; Sui Ning Ho: centre 63; Tiara Observatory, Tersch Enterprises: centre 24. Su Song clock top right 26, based on J. Christiansen, 1956.
All other pictures and illustrations provided by the authors.

Contents

Contrasts in Greatness

J. Tuzo Wilson

Director-General, Ontario Science Centre. Tuzo Wilson is a world-renowned geophysicist and major contributor to the theory of plate tectonics. A frequent visitor to China, he has written two popular books on China and was instrumental in the conception of this exhibition.

When westerners first visit China, they find Chinese customs strange and refer to China in such terms as "The Mysterious East." Those who know China better don't agree, but how did the Chinese acquire this false reputation for mystery?

The answer lies not in any basic difference between people, but in the development of China in almost complete isolation from the rest of the world throughout most of history. Hence, two regions often reached different solutions to common problems. To take two simple examples, everyone agrees that colours are inappropriate for mourning, but as an alternative the Chinese chose white while most others use black. Again, the Chinese eat with chopsticks, whereas others use their fingers or knives and forks. Writing illustrates a more fundamental difference. The Chinese developed their characters from simplified pictures while other races, from India westwards, use phonetic alphabets.

China is separated from the rest of the world by oceans, mountains and deserts.

Before the Arabs had begun to trade at Guangzhou (Canton), or Marco Polo had followed the Mongols across Asia, no direct communications with the outside world existed, only slow infiltration and trading from one intermediary to another. Chinese history records that only 150 mercenary soldiers reached northwest China from Rome and no Chinese got further west than the eastern shore of the Black Sea.

Communications within the rest of the old world were easier. Did not the Phoenicians explore Britain, Xerxes invade Greece, and Alexander campaign in India? Different as are the civilizations of Western and Eastern Europe, North Africa, the Near and Middle East and India, all parts knew something of the other parts.

These great territories—China and the rest of the world—apparently developed high technology, largely independently, often distinctively.

Two fundamental distinctions between these realms mark their approaches to government and religion. Until this century the Chinese never departed from their system of absolute rule by an emperor. True, the emperor lived in isolation and the power of weak emperors was shared with a well-organized bureaucracy, but the Chinese attempted no other system.

Secure under an emperor whose chief ceremonial function was to intercede with heaven, the Chinese could be ambivalent about religion. They had no exclusive belief in a supreme being, nor in any universal religion. A single individual might at the same time be a Buddhist, a Taoist and practise Confucian ethics.

Chinese attitudes towards travel and overseas colonization were conservative. Characteristically, it was not the Chinese, but Arabs, Mongols and Europeans who broke down barriers to communication and it was some of these same peoples who first established great overseas empires. This was not due to an inability on the part of the Chinese. It was the Chinese who first developed large seaworthy ships and gunpowder, invented the compass and had a good knowledge of astronomy, charts and navigation. Early in the fifteenth century they used these skills to send several fleets of large ships to India and East Africa, before the Europeans.

Previously they had bought back eu-calypts from Australia and they may have reached the Americas, but in each case they all returned, making no attempt to colonize or spread their empire beyond the limits of eastern and central Asia.

Differences even extended to their design of gardens. The Chinese garden is an idealization of wilderness as opposed to the idealization of cultivated land in gardens farther west. It is a place of hidden corners and limited views, planted with bamboo, gnarled cypress and pine trees, fantastically eroded rocks and only a few traditional flowers.

A curious effect of the last ice-age was that it killed most of the flowering plants of Europe and North America, but spared those of south central China. During the last three centuries, these glorious flowers, which the Chinese did not traditionally use in gardens, have been brought to the west to enrich our gardens with azaleas, rhododendrons, clematis, forsythia, camelias, perpetual roses, and many of the finest lilies as well as the plants of traditional Chinese gardens.

As this exhibition makes clear, the Chinese discovered many of the inventions we think of as our own, centuries before the rest of the world, but in spite of developing a stable economy, great engineering works, the making of steel, printing, paper money and a system of banking, they never had an industrial revolution. Perhaps this was because of their conservative system of government, or their success in mobilizing manpower, but for whatever reason the ancient Chinese never learned to use steam and synthetic power.

Nevertheless, for long periods between 200 B.C. and 200 A.D., the Chinese Empire rivalled Rome and, from 600 until 1500 A.D., they were the world's most advanced power, after which China entered a long period of decline. Should not study of the history of the only civilization which earlier achieved many of our own skills tell us something about whether China will rise again and what the future may hold for us and our continued prosperity?

Introduction

WENDY SNYDER MACNEIL.

Nathan Sivin
Professor of Chinese Culture and of the History of Science, University of Pennsylvania. Professor Sivin is the author of many books and articles on Chinese science.

As this exhibition makes clear for the case of China, the great ancient civilizations evolved their own sciences, based on their own views of the cosmos, the earth, the human body, and other aspects of nature and of man's relation to it. The major civilizations have been decisively influenced by each other at least since the New Stone Age, and the scientific and industrial revolutions of Europe are hardly thinkable without many earlier impulses from China, India, and Islam. Citizens of China and people of Chinese descent have had a hand in shaping every field of twentieth-century science and technology. Modern science can now be depicted accurately as a world enterprise, and China from early times to the present as a great contributor to that enterprise. Let me give a few examples.

The basic impulse of astronomy, in the several civilizations where it has been highly developed, has been to understand the regularities of the phenomena in the sky. Some, such as the phases of the moon, are so obviously regular that they could be predicted accurately two thousand years ago. Some are complicated, like the apparent wanderings of the planets among the stars, which were finally analyzed into combinations of simple motions. Some, such as the explosions of stars, reflect processes that we now understand well enough to belive that they follow regular laws, but not well enough to predict when and where they will occur. Most of the Chinese astronomy of which we have records was done in the Imperial Court, for it was the emperor's prerogative to issue the ephemerides–an almanac that forecast all the events in the sky that could be calculated in advance. Events that could not be predicted were recorded when they appeared, and interpreted as astrological warnings to the emperor of something amiss in the political realm. These records, usually detailed and precisely dated, have no counterpart in medieval Europe. They have been systematically studied in recent years to provide data on ancient supernova explosions that correspond to present-day sources of radiation, on the exact intervals between appearances of Halley's comet over the past two millenia, on cyclic changes in the visibility of sunspots, and on many other matters of theoretical interest in modern astronomy. Because the astrological records include happenings on the earth and in its atmosphere as well as in the sky, they have been used, for instance, to study cycles in the appearances of auroras, and to reconstruct in detail the earthquake history of many parts of China (a matter of concern not only to architects and planners, but to earth scientists attempting to predict earthquakes).

In medicine, another example, the traditional Chinese apothecary's shop, although very different from the health-and-beauty supermarkets of the contemporary urban west, resembles in many ways the shops of North America a century ago. But drugs–of animal and mineral origin as well as herbal– are not the whole story, for Chinese doctors generally combined them with prescriptions concerning diet, exercises, massage, and a number of therapies less familiar in the Occident such as acupuncture, which uses needles inserted in the flesh, and moxibustion, in which small cones of punk are burnt on the skin (or, to avoid burning the skin, it is merely warmed). The object of all these methods is to restore a balanced circulation throughout the body in harmony with the rhythms of the environment. This was consistently a holistic conception of health; even in cases of wounds and skin disorders the main concern was the effect upon the body as a whole. The best physicians treated the body as a whole, acting to strengthen its powers of recovery and to prevent the spread of damage. It is perhaps in this highly developed and well-documented tradition of attentiveness to the whole body, in its relations not only to its environment but to its emotional life, that Chinese medicine has the most to teach the west.

Pathbreaking approaches are less obvious in other fields of endeavour. In architecture, for instance, the elaborate systems of roof brackets distribute the weight of massive roofs supported by widely spaced wooden pillars, not by load-bearing walls. The flexibility of these bracket systems now appears responsible for the remarkable stability of the buildings in earthquakes. There was also the system of modular construction that, for at least a thousand years, related all the dimensions of massive palace buildings to the cross-section of one basic structural member.

In ceramics, the early perfection of porcelain was due not only to the availability of kaolin clay, but to the gradually perfected design of kilns that could efficiently maintain very high temperatures. This success influenced that of cast-iron production. High-temperature furnaces based in important respects on early ceramic kilns made cast iron, and the steel made from it since the fifth century B C , important commodities a couple of thousand years before the evolution of furnaces in Europe enabled large-scale production.

Savoured in an unhurried way and reflected upon, these examples, this book and the exhibition on which it is based can also help one to comprehend better the ideas and habits of mind that made possible the achievements so richly sampled here.

*"PRINTING, GUNPOWDER and the COMPASS:
these three inventions have already changed the
face of the entire world and the condition of things.
The first is concerned with learning, the second with
warfare and the third with navigation. The changes
in these three areas will give rise to innumerable
discoveries in other areas and no matter what
empire, religion or constellation or human affair, no
human influence will be as great as that of the
discovery of these mechanisms."*

Sir Francis Bacon,
17th Century English scientist

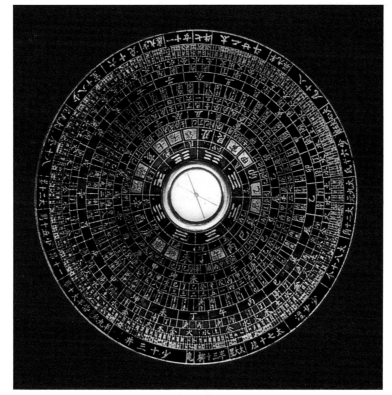

An astrological compass.

Magnetism and Exploration

The magnetic properties of the black iron ore called magnetite or lodestone have been known to the Chinese for at least 2,200 years. "Lodestone" (it was said) "is the mother of iron and will always draw her son back towards her." The first emperor of the Qin dynasty, Shi Huang Di, the powerful warrior who reunited China in 221 BC by ending the Warring States period and later became famous for building the Great Wall, ordered that the gates of the O-Fang palace be lined with magnetite to prevent anyone entering with iron weapons concealed in his robes.

At this time the Chinese also discovered the north-south pointing properties of lodestone and fashioned the world's first compass, the "south-governor." This was carved in the shape of a ladle and balanced on a round, bronze plate, representative of the Heavens, which was set within a square plate representative of the earth. The compass was engraved with 24 azimuth bearings and when the south-governor was spun it always came to rest with its handle pointing to the south.

The earliest reference to the use of a south-pointer as a direction finder was written in the 3rd century BC although its origins may be 300 years older: "When the people of Zheng go out to collect jade, they carry a south-pointer with them so as not to lose their way in the mountains."

Natural lodestone compasses were still being used in the 10th century AD but advances in technology during the 11th century led to the use of artificially induced magnetism. Two methods of making magnets were known at that time. The first involved polarizing pieces of iron by heating them in the earth's magnetic field. Thin strips of iron were cut into the shape of a fish, placed in a fire until they were red hot and then laid down north-south to cool. This magnetized the iron fish so that when they were floated in bowls of water their heads pointed south. The second method of inducing magnetism was to take an iron needle and rub it with a piece of lodestone, making the first true compass needle. From then on all that was needed was an improved method of suspension.

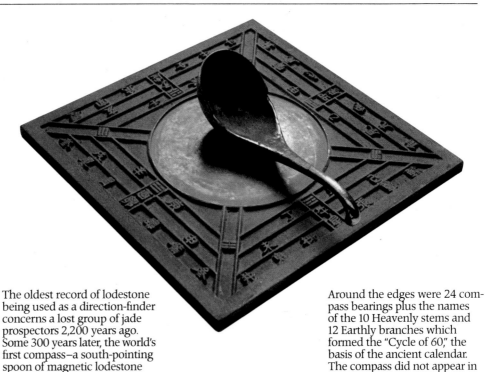

The oldest record of lodestone being used as a direction-finder concerns a lost group of jade prospectors 2,200 years ago. Some 300 years later, the world's first compass—a south-pointing spoon of magnetic lodestone balanced on a round, bronze plate within a square plate – was invented.

Around the edges were 24 compass bearings plus the names of the 10 Heavenly stems and 12 Earthly branches which formed the "Cycle of 60," the basis of the ancient calendar. The compass did not appear in the west until the 12th century AD.

Four ways to pivot a compass needle were described by Shen Kuo in his *Dream Pool Essays* of 900 years ago: floating it by pushing it through a slip of rush; balancing it on a fingernail or the rim of a bowl; hanging it from a silk thread. With the suspension method Shen Kuo made an instrument so sensitive he was able to detect magnetic declination—the difference between true and magnetic north. The ship's compass—a needle floating in a bowl marked with bearings—was invented in the 12th century. This led the way to the age of exploration.

In the 11th century AD, in *Dream Pool Essays* the scientist Shen Kuo described four ways of suspending a magnetic needle: pass it through a piece of rush of the kind used to make lamp-wicks so it can float on water; balance it on a fingernail; balance it on the rim of a bowl; suspend it by a single silken thread. With his invention of the silk thread suspension Shen Kuo created an instrument so sensitive he was able to detect the declination between true north and magnetic north 400 years before Columbus discovered it in the west.

The final stage of Chinese compass development was the appearance of the azimuth bearing pan marked with the 24 Chinese compass points which enclosed a bowl of water with a floating compass needle–much like a modern liquid-filled compass. These compasses were used until the 16th century when more convenient dry mountings were introduced.

The invention of the compass had an enormous impact upon the art of navigation. China's maritime history can be traced back 2,200 years but, before the invention of the compass, ships which tried to cross the broad oceans easily became lost in that vast expanse where sky and water meet without boundaries. It was very difficult either to reach an objective or to return home and once a ship was lost its crew risked ending up as no more than food for the sharks and fishes. Ancient seamen had navigated by the sun, moon and constellations but once they met cloud or rain it was almost impossible for them to stay on course. This was all changed when the water compass was introduced to navigation by China in the 12th century AD.

In 1958, near the city of Dalian in northeast China, several "needle bowls" were found in a Yuan dynasty tomb of the 13th century AD. In the centre of the bowls were painted the images of floating magnetic needles with the character for "needle" written underneath, showing that these were compass-bowls. To make it float, a compass needle was pushed through a piece of rush. Then it was laid on the water in the bowl to make a "water needle." By turning the compass bowl until the needle on the bottom aligned with the floating needle it was possible to determine the north-south direction. Thus the "south-pointing needle" pointed the way for the

sailor and the traveller on land regardless of fog, cloud or rain. The invention of this instrument enormously accelerated the development of nautical technology which in turn stimulated the development of the azimuth compass with its accurately marked-off compass bearings.

With the aid of the compass seamen gradually explored and set the navigation routes they called "needle roads." In the logs of the ancient mariners there is often the instruction: "At a certain place go according to such-and-such a needle," which referred to a set azimuth or compass bearing. The route formed by the connection of the needle points was the "needle road" which made navigation safer and more reliable and allowed sailors to lose sight of the shores of their homeland with some hope of seeing them again.

The invention of the compass led to a rapid increase in China's foreign trade. By the 12th and 13th centuries AD she was trading with more than 50 countries in Africa and Asia. China's peak of maritime greatness came with the voyages of Zheng He in the early 15th century. Between 1405

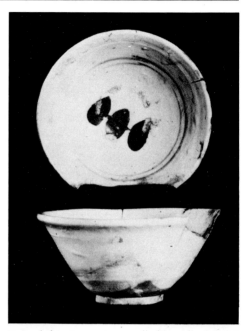

Several ships' compasses, called "needle- bowls," were found in a 13th century tomb of the Yuan dynasty at Dalian in northeast China in 1958. Once sailors had a compass, they could sail out of sight of land and expect to find their way back home.

The huge, nine-masted junks of the 15th century admiral Zheng He were five times larger than the ships of Columbus and Vasco da Gama. They were also safer, faster and required fewer men to sail them. The adoption of many of their features–the compass, rudder, water-tight compartments, efficient drainage pumps–made the great voyages of western exploration possible.

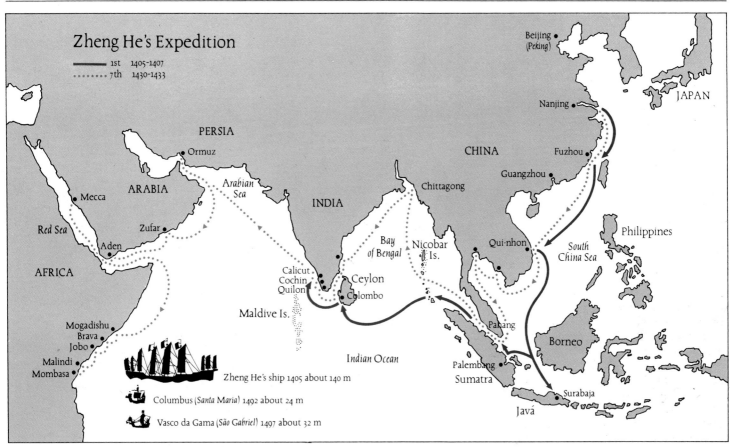

Zheng He's Expedition

— 1st 1405-1407
····· 7th 1430-1433

Zheng He's ship 1405 about 140 m

Columbus (Santa Maria) 1492 about 24 m

Vasco da Gama (São Gabriel) 1497 about 32 m

The Chinese sailed to Africa in 1433, 65 years before Vasco da Gama. They visited the chiefs, kings and sultans who ruled the coasts of all southern Asia. They brought back tributes of pearls, ivory, ostrich plumes, rhinoceros horn and a giraffe and a zebra for the Imperial zoo.

Navigation by the stars enabled the Chinese to determine their latitude at sea. The "Treatise on Military Affairs", written at the time of the great voyages of exploration 550 years ago, describes how this was done.

and 1433 he led seven fleets of huge junks into the western oceans. The largest of these consisted of more than 60 vessels with a crew of 27,000 men while the largest of his ships was 140 m long, the biggest in the world at that time. These were treasure fleets, laden with trade goods and gifts of porcelain, silk, bronze, iron, gold and silver for the chiefs, kings and sultans they met on their way. Zheng He visited Indochina, the archipelagos of Malaysia and Indonesia, India, Iran, Arabia and beyond to Mecca, birthplace of Islam, Somalia and Kenya on the east coast of Africa.

Zheng He did not only make a log. He handed down a map which records in detail his sea-routes with their anchorages, reefs and shoals from Nanjing, China to south-east Asia, India, Arabia and Africa.

As early as the Northern Song dynasty (960–1127 AD) when Chinese ships had long been plying the oceans of south-east Asia and India, many Arabs came to trade with China. Most of them rode in Chinese junks where they gradually mastered the secrets of the south-pointing needle. In the late 12th century the compass reached Europe where it provided a great stimulus to the exploration of the world. At the end of the 15th century, Vasco da Gama rounded the Cape of Good Hope, the southern tip of Africa, and arrived in India–nearly 100 years after Zheng He. In 1492 Columbus crossed the Atlantic and discovered for Europe the "new" world. None of these triumphs of navigation would have been possible without the compass which had been invented in China.

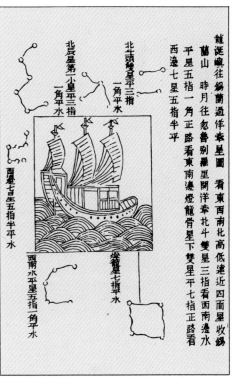

Gunpowder

In ancient times the emperors of China sent expeditions to the remotest parts of the empire and beyond in search of the men who were reputed to be immortals, in the hope of learning the secret of their "elixirs of eternal life." Taoist alchemists were brought to court to prepare drugs by heating cinnabar (mercuric sulphide), arsenic and other minerals which were thought to be the essential ingredients of any formula for immortality. No one succeeded in this quest but the search did encourage ceaseless experimentation.

The Chinese alchemists were working with sulphur and saltpetre by the 1st century BC and during the course of their experiments many fires were started. By the 8th century AD, in the mid-Tang dynasty, the potentialities of these substances when combined with charcoal were realized as the Chinese discovered an explosive mixture which they still call *huo yao* ("fire medicine") which came to be known in the west as gunpowder.

When saltpetre (potassium nitrate), sulphur and charcoal are mixed into black powder and ignited, the three ingredients react violently and emit great heat. Originally the three constituents were used separately as medicines. Sulphur was used to treat skin diseases (as it still is) while saltpetre was used to dispel fevers, treat stomach ailments and to disperse internal accumulations of blood. As recently as the 16th century gunpowder was still classified as a medicine because of its use in treating: "ringworm sores, insects, eczema and pestilence," hence the retention of the name "fire medicine."

Within a few years of its discovery gunpowder was put to use in warfare. In 1044 Zeng Gongliang wrote a military encyclopaedia, the *Wu Jing Zong Yao (Compendium of the Most Important Military Techniques)* which included the oldest recorded formula for gunpowder. It also details the formulae for poison smoke-grenades and spiked pottery firebombs as well as gunpowder for cannon. By the 12th century the first guns were in use for the precision discharge of arrows. Bamboo was used to make the first gun barrels, packed with gunpowder and fired by a fuse. In 1332, the world's first bronze cannon was made, a

Gunpowder–called "fire medicine"–blew up many laboratories from 100 BC onwards as alchemists heated mixtures of charcoal, sulphur and saltpetre in their search for the secret of eternal life. By the 8th century AD, it was used in war but the old name stuck. "Fire medicine" was still prescribed 400 years ago. China's discovery of gunpowder was helped by an abundance of natural saltpetre. In the 13th century, the secret reached Europe, where saltpetre for gunpowder was made by fermenting urine. This was done in pits where the saltpetre was scraped off the walls. Despite its late arrival on the scene, gunpowder had a greater effect on history in Europe than in China.

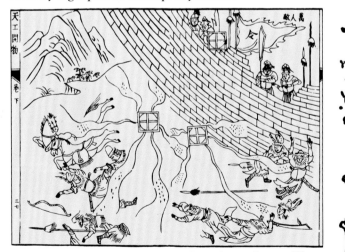

Raiders attacking the Great Wall are shown being driven off by grenades belching flames and poisonous smoke. They contained arsenic, poisonous plants, irritating oils and other unpleasant substances that could penetrate cracks in armour, cause choking and blister the skin. The men firing the bombs were advised to "suck black feathers and liquorice." Toxic substances were found to have other uses. The Chinese learned how to fumigate ships and buildings by burning sulphur inside them to drive out the vermin.

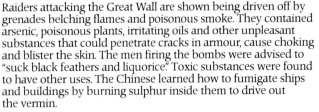

A 13th century flame-thrower that also worked like a shotgun. The bamboo barrel was filled with a fiery gunpowder mixture and tiny pellets called "seeds." These shot out in a blast of flame when the handle was forced into the barrel.

broad blunderbuss. This weapon is now on display in the Chinese History Museum in Beijing.

When gunpowder was introduced to the west it was mostly used in explosive bombs and mines. These things existed in China but there the main emphasis was on rockets and fire-weapons. More than thirty kinds of fire-arrow were developed between the invention of gunpowder and the 17th century. One of these, the "flying-bird" rocket was shaped like a crow. Its body was plaited from thin strips of bamboo and packed with gunpowder. Four pipes issued from the tail of the bird-rocket which had a range of 300 metres. It was an incendiary weapon that could be used to set an enemy's camp on fire or to burn his ships.

The Chinese also invented the world's first two-stage rocket, the "fire-dragon." When the gunpowder in the four rockets of the dragon's main stage was burnt up it ignited many small fire-arrows in its belly, causing them to shoot out of the fire dragon's mouth. These rockets were used in naval warfare where they looked like "fire-dragons" coming across the water.

The principle of these ancient rockets was the same as that which drives the rockets of today. Ignition of the gunpowder created a high temperature and an enormous pressure of gas. When this gas was allowed to escape at the rear the reaction propelled the rocket forward at high speed.

During the 12th century gunpowder was first used in firecrackers and fireworks in the celebration of festivals. A particularly elaborate example was the box-lantern. This was a multilayered, many-sided firework about one metre high. Inside it were folded fire-resistant paper illustrations of folk-tales, characters from plays and flowers. When the box-lantern was hung in a high place and ignited it exploded layer by layer so that the story gradually unfolded in whirling spark trails amidst a sea of light.

Gunpowder and firearms, which were to have a tremendous impact on western history, came to Europe via trade routes and the westward campaigns of the Mongol armies, finally arriving in the 13th century.

"Bees' Nest" multiple rocket launchers fired 32-100 fire arrows covered with gunpowder and tar. Mounted on wheelbarrows, they were light, mobile and deadly. The armies of the 14th-17th centuries preferred them to the cannon used in the west which were less useful against wooden targets.

A "Box Lantern" explodes to reveal flowers and folk characters in a shower of sparks. Fireworks are as old as gunpowder itself; like firearms, they were used in the time of the Vikings. In fact, the Chinese were exploding bits of bamboo by throwing them into a fire to make firecrackers long before they had gunpowder. Today, the making of firework displays is an exacting 1,300-year-old science and a great art.

As early as the 17th century, bombs were used to wage war on China's capricious climate. This bomb from Guizhou was fired into hail clouds to turn them into rain. The technique may not have worked but it was on the right track. Today, attempts to suppress hail formation with silver iodide crystals dropped or fired from aircraft are quite common.

This bird bomb had a woven bamboo body packed with gunpowder. Four rockets protruded from its tail. With a range of 300 m, it could swoop down on an enemy, burning his camp or his ships.

Papermaking

Without paper and printing human knowledge could not be preserved or disseminated, nor could humanity enjoy scientific and cultural advancement. Newspapers, letters, drawings, photographs, government and historical records, scientific papers–none would be possible without the invention of paper and printing, China's major contributions to the progress of world civilization.

Before the invention of writing man used to tie knots in rope to aid his memory and to help in the mental recording of events. About 6,000 years ago simple symbols were first used, which later became pictographs–crude drawings of objects and actions. Before the invention of paper, these pictographs were scratched on animal bones or tortoise shells–the "oracle bones" of early Chinese divination and record-keeping–engraved on pieces of stone or cast in bronze vessels. But these media were difficult to use and none was suitable for everyday purposes.

About 2,400 years ago *jiandu* were invented, strips of bamboo *(jian)* or wood *(du)* scraped flat and smooth so they could be written on. Each strip could hold a column of about 20 characters. When the strips were joined together they formed books called *ce*. 冊 Today this character, a pictograph clearly derived from the form of these bamboo books, is used to refer to a volume in a set of books. These bamboo books were a lot more convenient than animal bones or tortoise shells but they were still cumbersome and heavy, difficult to carry about and to store. It is recorded that Qin Shi Huang Di (the first emperor of the Qin dynasty who reunited China by ending the Warring States period in 221 BC and went on to build the Great Wall) attended personally to all the affairs of state and read more than 120 *jin* (more than 25 kg) of government documents each day, so we can imagine how unwieldy these *jiandu* must have been!

The Chinese were the first people to practise silk culture and silk weaving and from the 5th century BC they were using silk for writing and painting and rolling it up into scrolls. Silk made writing and reading much easier but it was extremely expensive. Only the emperor and his highest civil

Before they invented paper the Chinese wrote on bones. These inscriptions guided Imperial policy and recorded astronomical and historic events 3,000 years ago. Modern Chinese characters evolved from these ancient pictographs. While this was happening, the Babylonians of the Middle East were writing on clay tablets.

About 2,400 years ago the Chinese wrote on strips of bamboo or wood. These strips, which could be sewn into books, set the style of vertical writing. During this same period, the Egyptians were writing on papyrus: coarse sheets of matted reed.

Papermakers of the Han dynasty work beside a river 1,900 years ago. The process, announced to the emperor by Cai Lun in 105 AD, was the result of years of experiment. Paper transformed the arts in China. It led to the birth of watercolour painting and calligraphy with ink and brush, and encouraged the development of printing.

and military officials could afford it. For this reason silk was never used as commonly as the bamboo or wooden slips. Nevertheless, it was silk technology that would provide the clue that led to the invention of paper.

Before cotton was brought to China the people usually wore clothing made of silk or linen. For protection against the cold jackets and trousers could be quilted with silk wadding. This was obtained by steaming and boiling the silkworm cocoons then stretching them out on bamboo racks where they were repeatedly rinsed and beaten. When the wadding was lifted off the racks a very thin layer of silk floss was left behind. People tried to use this for writing. It was the accidental manufacture of this silk floss paper that pointed the way towards the manufacture of paper from cheap materials such as plant fibres.

Cai Lun–
The Invention of Papermaking

Cai Lun, who died in 121 AD, lived during the later Han dynasty. While he was still a child he was made a palace eunuch and in time he was promoted, first to Privy Counsellor in attendance on the emperor and later to Inspector of Public Works in charge of the emperor's factories. This post put him in touch with outstanding workmen from every region of China. Their skills were to have a profound impact upon him. Through careful study and painstaking analysis of the accumulated experience of the masses, Cai Lun and the Imperial workmen finally succeeded in making an economical and practical paper. In 105 AD Cai Lun reported this achievement to the Emperor He Di and presented him with the paper they had fabricated, thereby earning the emperor's praise and esteem.

The art of papermaking soon spread to every part of China, bringing about the rise of the papermaking industry. Now, for the first time in the history of the world, people could produce and afford to use paper in large quantities. The impact on the spread of civilization was incalculable.

The new paper was manufactured by taking tree bark, remnants of hemp, linen rags and old fish nets and shredding them, then boiling them and pounding them until they were reduced to a soggy, fibrous pulp. After the fibres were washed they were dispersed in a water-filled vat. This

Handmade paper is still an important Chinese industry whose techniques have hardly changed in 1,900 years. Plant fibres are chopped finely, ground up and mixed with mucilage which will bind the fibres together. The pulp is dispersed in water and lifted out as a thin sheet on a mesh screen. This sheet is then squeezed in a press to remove most of the water before the paper is dried. Different additives and finishes characterize hundreds of papers made according to principles which are also basic to Canada's highly automated paper industry.

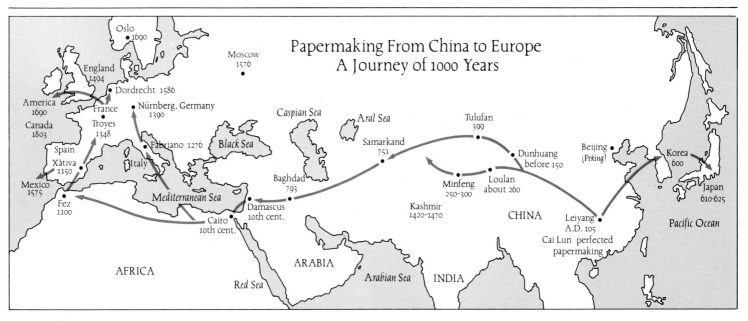

Papermaking From China to Europe
A Journey of 1000 Years

When the Chinese invented paper 1,900 years ago the Egyptians were still using sheets of coarse, matted papyrus reed and Europe was using costly parchment made from animal skins. In 610 AD, paper was taken to Japan by a Korean Buddhist monk. In 751 a Chinese army was defeated at the Talas River in central Asia. Among the prisoners were papermakers who settled in Samarkand. By the 12th century there were paper-mills throughout the Islamic world and in 1150 the craft arrived in Spain. From there, it spread across Europe and in 1575 the history of the paper industry in the Americas began with the building of the first Spanish paper-mill in the New World.

solution was then strained over fine mesh screens which held back the fibres in even sheets. The pulp, on the screens, dried to form paper. This 1,900-year-old paper-making process is essentially the same as that used in today's highly advanced paper-making industry.

China's Exquisite "Special Process" and "Speciality" Papers

The invention of cheap paper provided a tremendous spur to the twin arts of painting and calligraphy in China and this, in turn, hastened further developments and improvements in papermaking technology. Paper of every description was produced. Some bore the names of the materials from which they were made: hemp, bark, composite, reprocessed; while others were identified by their finish: water-ripple, dyed, gold and silver pattern, gold tracery. Some were named by their intended use: window paper, wallpaper, Imperial Edict paper, paper for copying Buddhist sutras, painting or sketch paper. There was also paper that took its name from its place of origin: Jiajiang from Sichuan, Danzhai from Guizhou, Xuan from Anhui—each a fragrant bloom in the paper-user's eye!

The importance of paper in Chinese culture may be exemplified by a close look at Xuan paper. Superficially, it looks like ordinary white paper but its smoothness and pliancy, its fine grain and even thinness, its whiteness and durability and its superb ink-absorbing qualities combine to make it quite remarkable. It is especially suited to Chinese ink-wash painting and calligraphy. The special richness that Xuan paper imparts to ink is largely a consequence of the raw materials used–a special tree bark and rice straw–and the manner of its fabrication. From selection of raw materials to the drying stage there are 18 manufacturing sequences involving more than 100 operations spread over more than 300 working days. It has been said, understandably, that the process depends upon the "combined workings of fire and water and the brilliance of the sun and the moon"!

Xuan paper exists in three basic types made with the addition of cotton, apricot or white bark. Addition of gold or silver dust produces a total of 90 varieties of converted papers e.g. "cold gold," "tiger-skin," "golden paint" and "cicada coat" Xuan. It may be used for calligraphy, painting, watercolour block-printing, folding fan faces and folk-art paper-cuts.

Xuan paper has a long history. At the turn of the 10th century, towards the end of the Tang dynasty, it was designated as a local speciality to be brought to the Imperial Court as tribute. It took its place beside the *Hu* writing-brush from Huzhou in Zhejiang province, the *Duan* ink-stone from Duanxi in Guandong province and the *Hui* ink-stick from Huizhou in Anhui province as one of the "Four Treasures of the Study" which were cherished by writers, scholars, painters and calligraphers.

Before the Chinese discovered paper the ancient world wrote as best it could on bones, tortoise shells, stone, metal, wood, bamboo and silk. In the west the Egyptians had used bark, palm leaves, papyrus made from matted and beaten reeds (which gave a very rough kind of paper) and parchment made from split, stretched and dried sheepskin. None of these could match Chinese paper for cheapness and smoothness; consequently, the west lagged far behind China in literacy until recent times.

Around the beginning of the 3rd century AD paper spread to Korea and Vietnam and from Korea to Japan. In 285 AD a scholar by name of Wang Ren from the Paekche kingdom of Korea carried the *Analects* and other works of Confucius to Japan—handwritten copies on paper.

In 610 AD a Korean priest, Tamjing, went to Japan and taught the Japanese the techniques of paper and ink-making that he had learned in China. Under the patronage of Prince Shotoku paper-mills were soon established in Japan. Towards the end of the 7th century papermaking reached India, Nepal, Pakistan and Bangladesh. The technology then spread to the west.

In 751 AD the Tang army was defeated at the Talas River by the powerful army of the recently created Islamic Empire. Among the many Chinese prisoners were some papermakers who were taken to the city of Samarkand where they were allowed to continue their trade which they passed on to their captors. From the mid-8th to the 11th century paper mills were established throughout the Asian and African territories of Islam.

In 1150 the technique spread to Europe with the establishment of the first paper factory in Spain from whence it spread to France, Italy and the rest of Europe. In 1575 the first paper mill was set up in North America. By the 19th century China's invention was known all over the world–living proof of the intelligence and creativity of the working people of ancient China!

A New Year wood-block print: "Eating Crabs on the Causeway." Mass copying of designs from carved wooden blocks dates back 1,400 years in both east and west but the invention of paper stimulated the craft enormously in China.

Wood-block printing on paper and printing with movable type were pioneered while western scribes were still copying manuscripts by hand on parchment.

Calligraphy, painting and poetry are intertwined arts, combining the ability to capture nature with brush and ink and to write a poetic description of the scene in flowing script. None of these arts would be possible without the "Four Treasures of the Study": the *Hu* brush, *Hui* inkstick, *Duan* inkstone and *Xuan* paper.

Printing

Chinese wood-block printing derived from the carving of signature seals in jade and other hard stones. The oldest extant specimens of signature seals are the two seals which were found in the ruins of Anyang, one of the capitals of the Shang dynasty (16th–11th centuries BC). Seals became particularly numerous during the Han dynasty, 800 years after the fall of Shang.

The carving of a printing block begins with the writing out of the desired text in the appropriate style of calligraphy. This is done on a piece of paper which is then transferred, face down on to the smooth face of a block of hardwood. The background is carved away, leaving the reversed characters in relief. Ink is spread evenly over the block, then a sheet of paper is laid over it and brushed down lightly. The characters are thus printed, correctly oriented on the paper. This technique was used to print drawings as well as writing.

The oldest evidence for the existence of wood-block printing dates back to the early Tang dynasty, 7th century AD. The first printed works included almanacs, medical texts, dictionaries and Buddhist images. The Buddhists, who were gaining strength in China at this time, were the first to realize the potential of printing for reaching the masses when the priest Xuan Zang mass-produced printed images of the Bodhisattva of Universal Sagacity and had them distributed to the four corners of the empire. Later in the Tang dynasty, in 835 AD, Feng Su, Provincial Military Governor of Eastern Sichuan presented a report to the emperor. It mentioned that calendars had been printed privately all over the country before the official calendar had been published. This shows that printing had spread to several areas, including Sichuan, Shaanxi, Henan and Jiangxi, apart from the major printing centres at the Tang capital Changan (modern Xi'an) and Chengdu in Sichuan.

In 1900 a great quantity of ancient writings was found hidden in a recess of one of the Caves of the Thousand Buddhas at Dunhuang in Gansu province. Among these scrolls was an undamaged copy of the "Diamond Sutra" with an illus-

A maker of signature seals carves into hard stone to leave the characters of his customer's name in relief. Seals have authenticated Chinese documents for more than 3,000 years. Until 600 BC most of them were carved into the stone but today they are usually left in relief. This is the origin of the idea of printing.

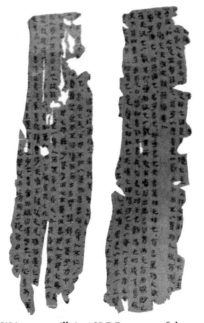

Written on silk in 168 BC, a copy of the Taoist classic of Lao Zi found in 1973. This writing material was made from the thin, matted waste left over from silk manufacture but it was still expensive. Other materials, like bamboo, bone and the Egyptian papyrus or parchment animal skins used in the west, were too rough to print on. The invention of paper in 105 AD would eliminate both of these problems.

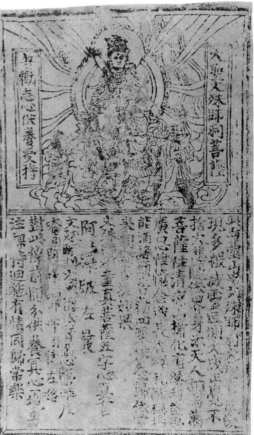

A portrait of the Wen Shu Shi Li Bodhisattva, a Buddhist saint, printed from a single wood-block about half a century after the 868 AD production of the world's first printed book. The idea of wood-block printing was known in both east and west but only China had paper: cheap, smooth and ideal for the mass production of books and tracts like this.

tration of the Buddha preaching at the beginning and at the end a clear inscription of the date with the dedication: "For universal free distribution by Wang Jie to perpetuate the memory of his parents, 15th day of the 4th month of the 9th year of the Xian Tong reign period of the Tang emperor." That was 868 AD–the world's oldest known printed book! The calligraphy on the six blocks used to print the scroll, which is nearly 5 m long, was carved with a level of proficiency which indicates that printing techniques had already attained a state of maturity by this time.

In 1944, a sheet of the Dharani Sutra Incantations was discovered in a Tang dynasty tomb in an eastern suburb of Chengdu. The Buddhist prayer had been printed by the Bian family of Longzhi district. This page has a Buddhist image and an exorcism printed in Sanskrit. This is the earliest example of Chinese printing currently residing in the Chinese History Museum in Beijing.

In the 10th century AD, by which time carved block printing had attained a high level of refinement, the imperial court undertook a massive project–the printing of the major classics. The chief minister at this time was Feng Dao but he preferred to be known as Chang Le Lao–the "Eternally Happy Elder." Under his leadership, the Imperial Academy supervised the project for 22 years. First they re-interpreted and corrected the official versions of the Confucian classics that had to be studied by the students who hoped to pass the gruelling civil-service examinations. Then they printed the Nine Classics and the other works. These versions became definitive and anyone who wished to study them could either buy copies of the books or hire the blocks so they might have them printed for themselves. This was the first large scale printing of books and it had a great influence on the history of printing in China. Following the lead of the government, the private printing and sale of books became very popular.

During the Song dynasty (960-1279 AD) imperial patronage encouraged the printing of a great quantity of books by the central and local governments so that wood-block printing entered a golden age. In 971 AD the Song emperor Tai Zu authorized printers in Chengdu, capital of

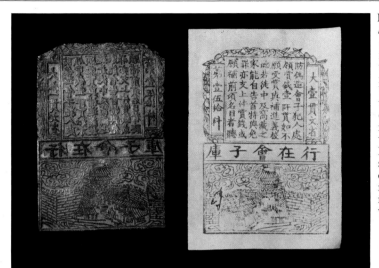

Paper money, called *hui zi* ("pocket money"), was first printed in 1005 AD, when the west was still doing most of its trade by barter. This 12th century copper plate is engraved with an intricate design to prevent counterfeiting. It was made in the southern Song capital of Hangzhou. Copper is ideal for long printing runs which quickly wear out wood-blocks.

A stone tablet with a design engraved on it is covered with moistened rice paper, then gently stamped with an inked pad to make a rubbing. Carved stone tablets like this, 2,000 or more years old, may hold works of ancient philosophy or scenes of historical events or everyday life. Before the invention of printing this was the only cheap way of acquiring copies of works like the Confucian classics, carved in stone for posterity. The wearing out of these stones spurred their duplication in the form of printing plates in the 11th century AD.

Printing with movable type was invented by Bi Sheng around 1045 AD. Separate ceramic characters were positioned in wax on a metal tray. The wax was then heated and the characters levelled. When the wax cooled, the characters were firmly set. To re-set, the tray was simply heated again. This was about 400 years before Gutenberg's Bible of 1445. None of Bi Sheng's type has survived. This reproduction is based on a description in the scientific *Dreampool Essays* written in Bi Sheng's time.

Sichuan province, to compile the Buddhist scriptures. This work, the *Tripitaka* has a total of 5,048 'chapters' *(juan)* and the carving of its 130,000 blocks took 12 years to complete. When it was finished, copies were presented by the government to the major monasteries of the empire and also to friendly neighbouring countries. Later works printed during the Song dynasty became highly valued by book collectors. They include the *Tai Ping Yu Lan (Imperially Reviewed Encyclopaedia of the Taiping Era), Wen Yuan Ying Hua* (a collection of outstanding writings–mostly literary), *Tai Ping Guang Ji (Wide Gleanings Made in the Taiping Era*–an encyclopaedia of material not found in the orthodox works) and the *Ce Fu Yuan Gui (Outstanding Models from the Storehouse of Literature)*.

In addition to its massive literary output, the Song dynasty was also responsible for printing the world's first paper money and, incidentally, for producing with it the world's first paper-led economic inflation. That was in 1005 AD when the paper money called *jiao zi* ("pocket money") was first distributed. When the Song was partially defeated by the Mongols at the beginning of the 12th century and forced to set up a new capital in the south at Hangzhou, it issued a great quantity of paper money called *hui zi* after the Hui Zi treasury. The Hui Zi mint employed 1,200 people of whom more than 200 were printers. Bronze plates were used to print the paper money, engraved then as now with intricate designs to render counterfeiting difficult. One plate from the 12th century still exists.

Later developments in printing technology included multi-colour printing and the *dou ban* technique. During the Yuan dynasty in the 14th century AD colour prints were made for the first time by carving several blocks of the same size for each plate, one block for each colour. The process began with just two colours but later increased to seven. *Dou ban* printing developed from the multiple block technique invented in the Yuan but the result was more exquisite and it was mainly used for printing copies of paintings. The block was divided into several small pieces according to colour. For each colour a separate printing was done on the same piece of paper. In the 17th century Hu Zhengyan used the *dou ban* method to

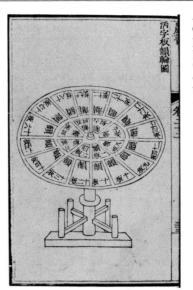

A pair of rotating trays for the storage of thousands of type characters was described by Wang Zhen in a chapter on printing in his *Book of Agriculture* of 1313 AD. Although printing was invented in China, Chinese has never been easy to adapt to it. Wang Zhen's device for storing the characters according to their rhymes made typesetting so fast that in 1298 AD he was able to print his 100-volume *Record of Jingde County* in less than one month.

The *Works of Yan Lugong*, printed with movable bronze type during the Jia Jing. reign period of the Ming dynasty, 1522-1566 (the time of Henry VIII). Bronze type was used in China from the 14th to the 19th centuries. Metal type was more durable than wood or ceramic. In Europe, printers were using cast lead type invented by Gutenberg in the mid-15th century.

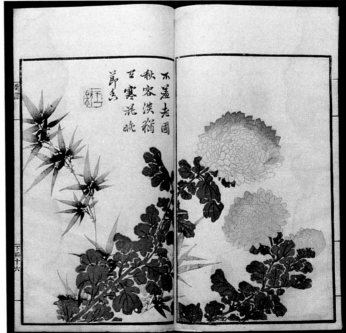

The *Mustard Seed Garden* manual for the teaching of painting was printed in 1701. Multi-colour, multiple woodblock printing was invented in China in the 14th century. Each colour was printed by a separate block. For instance, one block might carry just the stem and the leaves or the petals but no other part of the final flower design. These prints were often masterpieces both of art and the observation of nature. In Europe, until the invention of lithography in 1798, prints were sold "penny plain and twopence coloured" –by hand.

print a collection of paintings called *Ten Bamboo Studio Album of Paintings*. It was at this time that coloured New Year woodcuts originated among the people. The most famous of these came from Taohuawu near Suzhou and Yangliuqing near Tianjin. In addition to the wood-block print, Yangliuqing New Year woodcuts were also decorated with additions of coloured powders.

Printing with movable type was invented by Bi Sheng between 1041-1048 in the Song dynasty. This was recorded by Shen Kuo in his *Meng Xi Bi Tan (Dream Pool Essays)* a work on natural science and technology (see MAGNETISM AND THE COMPASS). Bi Sheng fashioned each character out of clay and hardened them by firing. When it was time to print, the type was set in a mixture of resin, wax and paper ash spread on a metal platen. Before printing, the platen with the type set was heated to melt the mixture; then the characters were flattened and smoothed. Once the platen had cooled it could be used as a printing plate. To release the type for further use the platen needed only to be heated again.

In the 13th and 14th centuries, during the Yuan dynasty, the agriculturalist Wang Zhen made a great contribution to the progress of movable type printing when he appended a chapter: "To Make and Print with Movable Type" to his *Book of Agriculture*. In this he described how, during the years 1297/98 he made more than 30,000 pieces of movable type out of wood and printed the 100-volume *Jingde Xian Zhi (Record of Jingde County)* which has 60,000 characters. The work took him less than one month! An important part of the secret of his astonishing speed was his use of a pair of rotating trays containing the fonts of movable type stored according to their rhymes. The typesetter sat between these trays, turned them to find the characters he wanted and set them in the platen on the bench in front of him. This made retrieval of the type very fast and easy.

Wang Zhen's chapter on printing concentrates on his experiments with the making of movable type, its setting and printing with it. It is the world's earliest treatise on the subject of movable-type

printing. After 1300 the use of movable type spread to areas north-west of China. A large quantity of movable type in the Uighur script has been found, substantially of the kind recommended by Wang Zhen, in the Dunhuang caves of Gansu province which were the hiding place of the Diamond Sutra.

China was also the first country to make and use movable metal type. This was first done in the 13th century, using tin. The earliest extant bronze type dates from 1490. In that year Hua Sui of Jiangsu province printed the *Song Zhu Chen Zou Yi (The Song Dynasty Ministers' Memorials to the Emperor)* and other works. After this the use of copper type became more common.

In 1726 the Qing government printed the *Gu Jin Tu Shu Ji Cheng (Encyclopaedia of Ancient and Present Day Books)*. This consisted of 5,200 'volumes' *(ce)* in 64 sections and is the largest work ever printed with movable copper type. The printing techniques invented in China spread to Japan and Korea and westward to Iran, Egypt and Europe.

When the printing block is inked, paper is laid over it and padded down. The sheet is then dropped into a slot to await the next block and a different colour. The bold brush-strokes of Chinese art are well suited to reproduction by printing. Love of nature and the subtle nuances of fine calligraphy encouraged the development of wood-block printing into a fine art that was preferred even for the reproduction of many written works.

Carefully aligning her paper over an inked block that carries a design carved in relief, this woman can print up to 3,000 copies. Separate blocks–as many as seven–are used for each of the colours, and great care has to be taken to ensure that they are properly aligned, otherwise the colours will overlap. Multiple block colour printing was invented in China in the 14th century AD.

Creativity in China

Hsio-yen Shih

Hsio-yen Shih is the former Director of the National Gallery, Ottawa and previously Curator of the Far Eastern Department of the Royal Ontario Museum.

A whole meal of meat and vegetables cooked in seconds with a Mongolian hot-pot–plates of varied tidbits seemingly infinite for the Cantonese tea-lunch; a padded peasant's jacket of blue cotton–the imperial dragon robe of embroidered brocade; a house cut out of loess earth deposited by the Yellow River in north-central China–bamboo scaffolding for the building of a concrete, glass and steel sky-scraper in Hong Kong; these are some Chinese answers to the human need for food, clothing and shelter. Do we contrast them here simply to show how different phenomena can be over the vast stretch of space and time that is China? Or, do these apparent oppositions share a special approach in abilities to make, invent, devise, fashion and produce–all definitions of creative acts–that is culturally distinctive? And why look for evidence of what is most valued in human endeavour through examples of such simple use?

If we think of creativity as mental activity stretching to discover and invent, as well as physical activity exerted to form new and/or better results, problems of everyday life may provide the greatest challenge. Their identification, analysis and solution can be tested by most people and at any point in time. We are, or should be, worried about energy conservation and the use of the world's natural resources. Consider, then, how economic and efficient the use of fuel is to warm both food and people when charcoal is placed in the centre compartment of the hotpot, or to ensure the sanitation of food with thorough heating in multi-levelled steamers. Examine, as well, the many possibilities of use in any natural material so that wastage is reduced and more varieties of service can be had from it. Judge, furthermore, the balance between expenditure of labour and its results for temporary or long-term gains. The cutting of food to smaller size for quicker cooking, the mixing of different food-stuffs for nutritional balance, and the transformation of eating into a communal event–all these are part of a creative process.

Whether we speculate on the examples given, ponder a museum's treasure of a bronze ceremonial vessel from China's first historic period (the Shang dynasty) or enjoy a porcelain tea-cup of the sort we can buy almost anywhere imported from the People's Republic of China today, we should recognize a particular attitude towards materials and techniques. Understanding the limitations of these resources may be one aspect of Chinese creativity, and by-passing of constraints by ingenuity and labour another. Often, appearance is deceiving–the bronze's massive dignity depends upon the malleability of the clay piece-moulds from which it was cast; the tea-cup's fragile prettiness belies the strength of its fabric in high-fired kaolin minerals. Is it an aesthetic or another more than functional concern that prompts the Chinese maker to push exploration of substance and its manipulation to extremes that hide or disguise its more obvious characteristics? And, how do we relate this view with the utility of so many Chinese inventions–not only the famous triumvirate of printing, gunpowder and the magnetic compass, but also the wheelbarrow, crank, driving-belt and many others?

One answer may be in the group participation necessary to much that China has created. Astronomical observation, seismographic recording and the compiling of pharmacopoeias depend as much on cumulative effort for their results, as do metal smelting and casting, ceramic mixing and firing, or silk extraction and weaving. Their effectivity is the greater for the contributions of many minds and bodies, and over a period of time. The idea that creativity leads to a single and complete act implies a final, immutable product. But, the perception that creativity is a process involving many elements in interaction permits change through modification or addition at any stage. A satisfactory solution to a problem can emerge and be retained; a problem can be reseen and a new direction of exploration initiated; or solutions can be reworked or refined. Over the many centuries in which Chinese were engaged in any particular sphere of activity, they produced a great variety of simple and complex results. From this multitude, we retain knowledge and use of the most efficient, amusing or impressive–one could describe as the most life-enhancing.

A Chinese emphasis on process in creativity may be responsible for less importance placed on the individual creator or the individual creative act. There are cultural heroes in Chinese mythology–as, for example, Fu Xi who is supposed to have invented writing, fishing and trapping or Shen Nong who is said to have introduced agriculture and commerce; but, they serve as symbols of the chronological stages in the evolution of society, rather than as idealizations of single impulses or acts of creativity. There are, also, individual names in Chinese history to whom specific inventions are attributed–as, for example, Cai Lun and paper in the 2nd century A.D. or Bi Sheng and movable type in the 11th; but, their contributions could be considered as improvements or adaptations of existing processes to new ends, silk to paper in the first case and ceramic plus metal fusion for the combination of durability and reversible process in the second.

The Western tradition retains an ideal of genius in the creative person; that is, a special and divinely given extra ability. In China, the twin endowments of talent and skill (one inborn and the other nurtured) are acknowledged, but not supra-human gifts, though exceptional achievement could be praised as partaking of "the spirit, the numinous, the divine" *(shen)*. But, *shen* is not equivalent to a Creator God. The nearest Chinese concept to the idea of a divine life-giver is in the "maker of things" *(zaowuje)* to whom the philosopher Zhuang Zi's fertile mind aspired. *Shen* is sometimes described as "the power" behind "the productive process" *(zaohua)*. The maker of things and the productive process are not so much inspired as activated by *shen.* Man's creativity is related to the cosmic productive process in most Chinese thinking. And, as the *Book of Changes (I-Jing)* comments, "The activity of the spirit shows itself in the totality of phenomenon; this is transformation *(bianhua)*." As Man's activity echoes that of the Universe, human creativity embraces all things and events leading to growth and change. And so, inherent in every material, technique and product is the possibility of different potentials to be discerned and released by man.

When China takes pride in its many contributions to world civilization, it acknowledges the creative activities of a host of anonymous workers throughout its history. This is a long-overdue recognition. The traditional Chinese bureaucratic state placed artisans below scholars and farmers in the social order, and above merchants only. The arts of poetry and its related field of music, calligraphy and painting, are exceptions to the rule of un-named creators in China, mainly because these were the province of scholars, deriving from and expanding the primacy of language and literature. Or, again, individuals with distinctive personalities abound for the creators of Chinese philosophy and statescraft. They, after all, formed the structure of government that gave first place to the scholar-administrator. To them, however, we owe much of what we know about China's development through their inexhaustible record-keeping.

Nevertheless, it is in an anonymous book distilling centuries of thought, albeit much commented upon by scholars Chinese and non-Chinese of both the past and present, that we find the essential Chinese statement on creativity.

That which lets now the dark, now the light appear is the Way. What issues from it is good, and that which brings it to completion is the individual nature. The man of humanity recognizes it and calls it humanity; the wise man recognizes it and calls it wisdom. People use it daily and are not aware of it, for the Way of the superior man is but rarely recognized. It manifests itself as humanity but conceals its workings. It gives life to all things, but is free from the anxieties of the sage. Its glorious power, its great field of action, are of all things the most sublime. It possesses everything in abundance: this is its great field of action. It renews everything daily; this is its glorious power. It produces and reproduces, and hence it is called change. *(from the Great Appendix to the Book of Changes.)*

Astronomy

Astronomy is one of the most ancient of China's sciences. Around 2600 BC the legendary "Yellow Emperor" Huang Di, established the 60 Year Cycle as the basis of the Chinese calendar. This was later adopted by the Xia, the first dynasty of China.

More than 1,000 years later, around 1400 BC during the Shang dynasty which replaced the Xia, the "Canon of the Emperor Yao" in the *Book of History, (Shang Shu)*, recorded how the stars were used to mark the changing of the seasons:

> "The day of medium length and the south culmination of the star Niao serve to adjust the middle of Spring. The day of greatest length and the south culmination of the star Huo serve to fix the middle of Summer. The night of medium length and the south culmination of the star Xu serve to adjust the middle of Autumn. The night of greatest length and the south culmination of the Star Mao serve to fix the middle of Winter."

The year was then set at 366 days and the four seasons were regulated by intercalary months. This ancient record marks the beginning of China's long and unbroken history of astronomy.

Almost all the emperors had a bureau of astronomers, four to twelve to a shift. By day they watched and recorded the movements of the sun, its eclipses and the appearance and disappearance of sunspots, etc. By night they observed the movements of the stars and the "Five Planets": Mercury, Venus, Mars, Jupiter, Saturn. They recorded the movements, phases and eclipses of the moon, meteor trails, the coming and going of planets and the explosion of stars into novae and supernovae. The observation of these phenomena became part of the official histories.

In the commentary to the *Spring and Autumn Annals*, which may have been written as long ago as the Warring States period, 475–221 BC, it is recorded that: "A comet entered the constellation *Bei Dou* (the Dipper) in autumn in the seventh month of the 14th year of the reign of Lord Wen of the state of Lu." This may be one of the earliest written records of Halley's comet. If this description is compared with the more recent records of the comet's appearance it is possible to determine that the plane of its orbit has

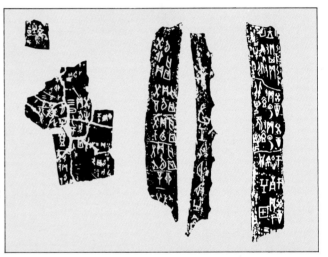

Scratched on bones, the oldest record in archaic Chinese script of solar and lunar eclipses, 3,000 years ago. The prediction of eclipses calmed the fears of those who thought the sun might never return. The ability to predict eclipses and the making of the calendar that was crucial for the regulation of China's agriculture were two of the most important sources of the emperor's power. These bones were inscribed by Imperial astronomers of the Shang dynasty when the ancient Britons were worshipping at the temple-observatory of Stonehenge.

The sun, blazing on fragments of clay pots made 5,000 years ago by neolithic farmers of the Yangshao culture, symbolizes a universal reverence for the sun as the source of all life. It was mankind's need to understand the sun's control of the seasons that led to the birth of astronomy.

The Chinese may have seen Halley's comet in 240 BC, 1,920 years before Halley. They recorded all appearances of this "brush star" to 1910. In the west, where comets were feared and often ignored as false evidence of cosmic imperfection, the record is scanty. Halley's comet streaks across the Bayeux tapestry which celebrated the Battle of Hastings of 1066 and Giotto painted it in 1301, confusing it with the Star of Bethlehem. The Chinese had no telescopes but their record of comets, sunspots and stellar explosions is the longest of any culture and has proved invaluable to modern astronomers in their study of the history of the universe.

altered since that time. From 240 BC to 1910 AD each of the 29 appearances of Halley's comet was recorded by Chinese astronomers. In 1973 a chart was found at Mawangdui in an early Han dynasty tomb (206 BC - 28 AD). Drawn on silk it depicts a variety of forms of comets – testifying to the precision of the observations of the ancient astronomers.

From the 11th century BC to the 18th century AD there are more than 90 records of novae and supernova explosions. The most famous of these was the supernova of 1054 AD in the constellation of Taurus: "In the morning the guest star arose in the east beside the star *Tian Guan*. In the daylight it looked like Venus. Light shot out in all directions and its colour was reddish white. After two years it faded." In the mid-19th century an Irish astronomer, the Earl of Rosse, equipped with a powerful telescope, discovered a crab-shaped nebula, a cloud of gas created by a supernova explosion, where the Chinese astronomers had observed the supernova 800 years earlier. In 1921 the nebula was discovered to be still expanding and we now know that it contains a pulsar which emits light and x-rays and gamma rays.

The principal role of the ancient astronomers was the establishment of a calendar by which society could regulate its agricultural production. The earliest evidence of the existence of calendars (apart from legend) is found inscribed on the "oracle bones" of the Shang dynasty dating from the 14th to 11th centuries BC.

The Chinese calendar is both lunar and solar with the length of the year determined by the sun and the months by the moon. The failure of the cycles of the moon to keep time with the earth's orbit around the sun was resolved by means of extra, intercalary, months and by arrangements of long and short months. As far back as 1400 BC, during the Shang dynasty, the tropical year was measured to be 365.25 days long.

Around 330 AD the astronomer Yu Xi compared the historical records of the winter solstice with his own observations. By comparing the position of the sun at the winter solstice with that of its nearest star and by matching his observations with those of his predecessor he was able to detect that the time of the solstice in relation to the stars had slowly shifted. The

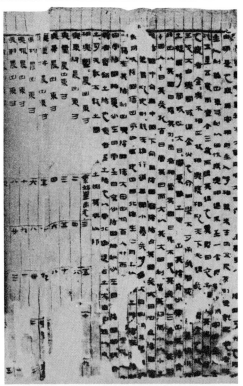

Recorded on silk in 170 BC, the movements of the "Five Planets" Mercury, Venus, Mars, Jupiter and Saturn. The time taken by each planet to orbit the sun was measured, from the 225 days of Venus to the 30 years of Saturn. The opposition of Mars, Jupiter and Saturn are also recorded – those times when each is exactly opposite the sun as seen from the Earth.

The astrological cycle of Rat, Ox, Tiger, Rabbit, Dragon, Snake, Horse, Goat, Monkey, Rooster, Dog and Pig is based on Jupiter's 12-year orbit of the sun – one of the movements recorded here. 1982 is the year of the Dog.

China's oldest calendar, the Cycle of 60, devised by the legendary Yellow Emperor more than 4,600 years ago, was made by combining the names of the mythical 12 Kings of Earth and 10 Kings of Heaven who first ruled the universe. The western year 1982 is 4678 of the 77th Cycle of 60. Later calendars for the timing of sacred rites and the control of agriculture were based on the sun and the moon which made them more complicated than the mainly solar western calendar.

The Crab Nebula, a luminous gas cloud 13 light years across and 6,500 light years distant was discovered through a telescope in 1839, by William Parsons. In 1054, a "guest star" had been observed in the same location by a Chinese astronomer. At its peak it was as bright as Venus. It remained visible by day for 23 days and at night for two years. We now know that this was a supernova, a gigantic stellar explosion and that the Crab Nebula is its remnant. The supernova was missed in the west.

sun had fallen a whole day behind. This phenomenon is called the precession of the equinoxes. Yu Xi calculated that the point of the winter solstice (and therefore of the summer solstice) shifts one degree to the west in 50 years. This means that the sun should return to its starting point against the stars in 18,000 years. (The Greek astronomer Hipparchus had discovered the precession of the equinoxes 450 years earlier but his calculation was less accurate than that of Yu Xi.) This discovery led to considerable refinement of the Chinese calendar.

In 1199 AD the astronomer Yang Zhongfu of the Song dynasty published his book about calendars, the *Tong Tian Li*. In this he became the first to use 365.2425 days as the length of the tropical year. This figure was confirmed about 100 years later by

Guo Shoujing of the Yuan dynasty after years of careful observation. Chinese calendrical science also involved the calculation of the positions of the sun, moon and five planets, the prediction of lunar and solar eclipses and determination of the lengths of the days and months as well as the years.

Chinese Astronomical Instruments

Among the most important Chinese astronomical instruments were·

Gnomons–vertical poles planted in the ground for measurement of the sun shadow to determine the length of the year and the seasons. *Armillaries*–nests of intersecting protractor rings with sighting tubes to measure the co-ordinates and to track the movements of the celestial bodies. *Clocks*–

for the timing of astronomical events.

The oldest remaining observatory in China is at Gaocheng, 15 km south of the ancient capital of Luoyang. This site was used as long ago as the Zhou dynasty (11th century BC) for measurement of the sun shadow at the equinoxes and solstices.

In 1276 AD, during the Yuan dynasty, the astronomer Guo Shoujing constructed an astronomical tower on this site. The gnomon within this tower is 4 *zhang* high (one *zhang* is about three metres), and is perpendicular to a shadow-scale 9.3 *zhang* long. This is grooved with a pair of channels filled with water to prove that the scale is perfectly horizontal. Two other improvements in the accuracy of this gnomon were a result of the huge size of the instrument and of a special invention of Guo Shoujing. This was a shadow definer placed on the

The date within the calendar month could be told from the phases of the moon.

← New period begins   New period begins   New period begins →

day 2   day 7   day 10   day 15   day 5   day 10   day 13

Moon and sun are both accommodated in the ancient lunar/solar calendar. Twenty-four, 15-day months make a year. Extra, intercalary months have to be inserted to keep moon and calendar in step and to round off the year to 365 days. The year begins when the new moon appears in the constellation of the tiger.

The calendar tower of the Imperial astronomer Guo Shoujing, built in 1276 AD, reflects the great importance of calendar making in Imperial China. It was used to determine the exact moment of the winter solstice–the shortest day of the year, when the sun shadow is longest. From this, the precise beginning of the new year was predicted. The shadow of the tower was cast on the horizontal scale which runs 31.2 m out from the base. The tower's great height created a long shadow. This and the shadow definer on the scale, made the instrument very accurate. The exact time of the solstice was marked and at night it was matched with the positions of the stars and the phase of the moon. The tower was built two years after the arrival of Marco Polo at the court of Kublai Khan, Emperor of China.

shadow-scale which enabled him to read off the length of the shadow from the tiny spot of light that shone onto the scale rather than the vague edge of the shadow at the tip of the gnomon. With this instrument the Yuan dynasty astronomers were able to improve the accuracy of their timing and prediction of the equinoxes and solstices and to refine further their calculations of the length of the year and the precession of the equinoxes.

The first armillary sphere for measuring the co-ordinates of the celestial bodies was built at the beginning of the 1st century AD during the Han dynasty. It was continually improved until it reached its final form in the Song dynasty some 1,000 years later, between the 10th and 11th centuries AD. The armillary sphere at the Zijin ("Purple") Mountain Observatory, Nanjing is based on a Song design but was built during the Ming dynasty between 1437 and 1442 AD. The armillary sphere could measure the co-ordinates of the "fixed" stars and track the courses of the sun, moon and planets. But it was complicated and with its system of interlocking rings could not measure the entire sky. In 1276 AD the Yuan dynasty astronomer Guo Shoujing (the builder of the great gnomon) designed an expanded or simplified armillary with fewer rings. The rings are also separated to make them easier to use and enabling them to be applied to a much greater area of sky. This instrument also has an equatorial mounting with its base parallel to the earth's equator and its vertical axis aligned with the poles, rather than the ecliptic mounting with its horizontal base aligned with sunrise and sunset. The latter was favoured in the west until the coming of the modern astronomical telescope when the Chinese equatorial mount became almost universal. The equatorial mount is preferable because it means that a star can be followed by moving the instrument in only one plane instead of the two planes necessary with the ecliptic mount. The choice of the equatorial mount by the Chinese reflected their interest in the rotation of the stars around the celestial pole rather than the rising and setting of the stars across the horizon which interested western astronomers.

Accurate measurement of time is crucial to the astronomer in the making of records that enable him to make predictions of

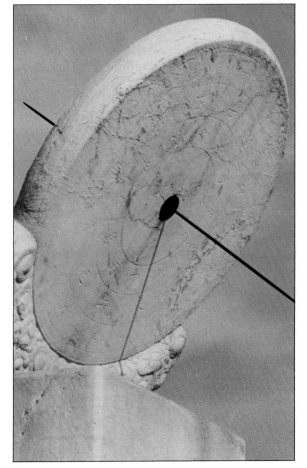

The simplified armillary of Guo Shoujing, built in 1276 AD, was a device for tracking the stars and planets and measuring their relative positions at different times of the year. Made of bronze, the instrument stands about two metres high. The small upper ring points toward the celestial pole around which the stars revolve. The other rings are fitted with sighting tubes and are marked in 365.25 degrees–equal to the number of days in the year. Erected at the Purple Mountain observatory, Nanjing, this instrument was used in calendar making. The armillary illustrated was built during the Ming dynasty, between 1437-1442 AD. It has a plane sundial rather than the square table sundial of Guo Shoujing's original armillary.

The sundial at the Imperial Palace, Beijing, built about 500 years ago, has an equatorial mount (the dial is parallel to the equator). The two gnomons, parallel to the earth's axis and pointing north and south, are used to tell the time in summer and winter respectively. At the spring and autumn equinoxes both sides of the dial are in shadow. The equatorial mount differs from the horizontal or vertical mount of western sundials in that it times equal hours. On horizontal or vertical dials the shadow moves more slowly early and late in the day, giving unequal hours.

cosmic events. It is also necessary if, as in ancient China, sacred rites that have to be performed according to the positions of the stars are to be timed accurately even when the stars are obscured by cloud. In China the ancient waterclock was refined to a degree of precision never achieved in the west. The *Lou Ke Jing*, a book on waterclocks, records: "Construction of waterclocks began in the days of the Yellow Emperor and they were improved during the Xia and Shang dynasties." This was between 4,600 and 3,000 years ago!

The earliest surviving waterclock was made around 113 BC during the Former Han dynasty. It was found in a tomb in Hebei province. This clock was relatively simple with just one reservoir which means that it ran fast when full and slow when nearly empty. Later clocks had cascades of four or five reservoirs which made the water flow more evenly and made their time-keeping more accurate. The great waterclock of the Song dynasty astronomer Su Song, built at the imperial observatory of the old capital at Kaifeng in 1068 AD, was a masterpiece of technology. The problem of accuracy was solved, as it was in the west 200 years later, by means of an escapement which broke the flow of energy from the clock drive into a series of discrete steps– the "ticks" of a mechanical clock.

Su Song's clock was housed in a tower 30 m high. It was driven by water flowing from a constant level tank onto the scoops of an escapement wheel 3.5 m in diameter. Two bronze bars, the "celestial balance," held back the scoop until it was quite full, then the escapement tripped and the wheel turned to bring the next scoop into place.

Elaborate gearing and transmission shafts connected the escapement to an armillary sphere on the top platform, a celestial globe in the upper chamber and an army of model men in the lower chamber who emerged through doors, ringing bells, striking gongs or beating drums and carrying placards which announced the time. Su Song's clock tower could tell the precise time of day or night and also indicate the positions of the heavenly bodies regardless of the weather.

Another invention of Su Song was the world's first planetarium. This was a spherical tent made of silk stretched over a bamboo frame. It was built around an axle that

A waterclock placed in a tomb 1,100 years ago is the oldest one yet found in China. As water dripped out of the can a scale attached to a float slid down and marked the time. A disadvantage of these early waterclocks was that they ran fast when full and slow when nearly empty.

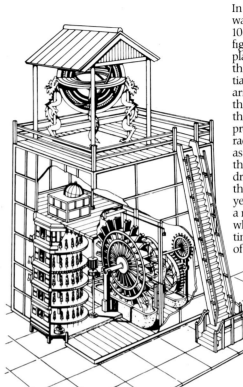

In Su Song's giant waterclock of 1068 AD, wooden figures carried placards telling the time, a celestial sphere and an armillary marked the positions of the stars. The problem of accuracy was solved, as it would be in the first weight-driven clocks in the west 200 years later, by a mechanism which broke up time into a series of precise "ticks."

The world's first planetarium, invented by Su Song nearly 900 years ago: a spherical silk tent with an observation chair hanging inside it. When the tent was closed, the chair was plunged into darkness. The tent turned on its axis which, like that of the earth, was inclined 23.5° to the vertical and, as it slowly rotated, light shone through pinholes pierced in the positions of the stars. It was used to train Imperial astronomers. Nothing like this "planisphere" would be seen in Europe until the 17th century when a similar device was presented to Peter the Great of Russia.

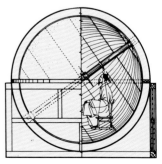

pivoted 23.5° to the vertical–just as the earth's axis is inclined to the plane of the solar system–the plane of the ecliptic. A chair was suspended inside the planetarium and when the observer sat in it, he was plunged into darkness except for pinpoints of light that came in through tiny holes pierced in the silk in the locations of the stars. When the planetarium was rotated it turned on its axis making the "stars" rotate about the observer exactly as they do in reality.

Nothing like the false sky of Su Song was seen in Europe until 1644–600 years later–when a planetarium was made for Peter the Great of Russia. The modern type of optical planetarium was invented by Zeiss of Germany in 1913.

Star Charts and Star Indexes

A vital role of the imperial astronomers was the measurement of the co-ordinates of the fixed stars and of the moving celestial bodies. The charts and indexes they have left are invaluable to the astronomical researcher and far more complete than comparable records made in the west. During the Warring States period in the 4th century BC, Gan De of the state of Qi and Shi Shen of the state of Wei both wrote books on the stars. Shi Shen listed the equatorial co-ordinates of 121 stars in China's earliest star index. Today this can only be found in copies made during the Tang dynasty during the first half of the 8th century AD.

Most ancient star charts belong to one of two types. One is more artistic and the other of more practical value. A star chart in scroll form was found in the caves at Dunhuang, Gansu Province, in the early part of this century. Drawn in 940 AD it shows 1,350 stars. The position of the sun is shown for each of the 12 months and the stars are divided into 12 groups along the region of the celestial equator. The images of the stars were cast from a cylinder to make the rectangular drawing of the equatorial region and from a sphere to make the circular drawing of the polar region with the pole star at the centre. These techniques were used to make charts which pre-dated Mercator's projection for depicting the curved surface of the earth on flat maps by 600 years. They are still used for drawing modern star charts.

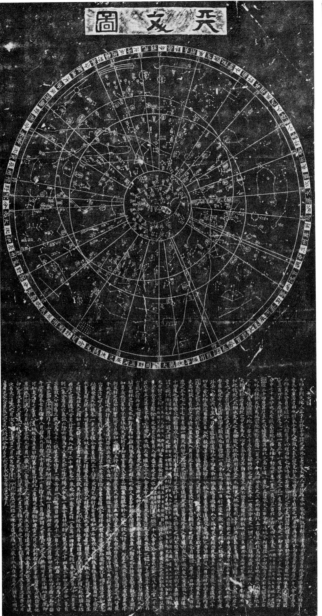

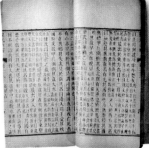

The discovery of Jupiter's moons in the 4th century BC by the astronomer Gan De was recalled in this book on astronomy 1,100 years later. The four satellites went unnoticed in the west until Galileo saw them through his telescope in the 17th century. Gan De's sole aid was a bamboo sighting tube to sharpen his night vision!

A map of the heavens carved on stone in Suzhou in 1247 shows the positions of 1,434 stars mapped between 1078 and 1085 AD. At the centre is the celestial north pole around which all the stars revolve. The closed spiral is the "road" followed by the moon as it passes through the 28 constellations called "lunar mansions" during the course of the year. Maps like this were used in both calendar making and astrology.

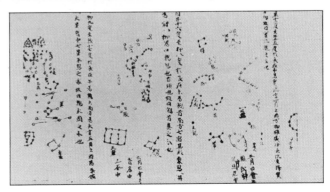

A scroll map made in 940 AD, showing the sun in relation to 1,350 stars for each of the 12 months of the year. It was found in a cave in Dunhuang, Gansu province, that was once occupied by Buddhist monks. The depiction of the curvature of the heavens in the form of a flat rectangle predated Mercator's projection for drawing maps by 600 years!

Mechanics

During their more than 4,000 years of civilization, the Chinese people have invented all kinds of machines to aid them in the pursuit of improved production and a better livelihood.

Irrigation probably began in China, as elsewhere, with peasant farmers carrying water to their fields in jars on their shoulders. But this consumed both time and labour. While the rivers were being tamed and led in irrigation canals to the fields that needed watering, machines were invented to make the job of transferring water to the soil easier. The first of these was the "well-sweep" which appeared between the 8th and 5th centuries BC. In this machine a bucket was hung on a rope from one end of a counterpoise beam which was balanced at the other end by a heavy stone. With this machine the back-straining task of hauling buckets of water up and out of a well or irrigation ditch and swinging them over to the field was made much easier.

In the 3rd century AD the "dragon backbone water machine" *(long gu shui che)* was introduced. It consisted of a trough running up from a river or irrigation canal to a ditch along the edge of a field. A wooden chain ran through the trough and around a pair of wheels, one at the upper and one at the lower end. Wooden boards, or pallets, were attached to the links of the chain, cut to fit snugly within the trough. Foot-operated cranks on the upper wheel allowed two men to turn it and draw water up from the lower level, raising water on the pallets. It was the appearance of the wooden chain with the pallets sticking out of it that gave the machine its name. With the dragon backbone water machine a pair of farmers could raise water 5 m onto their land. Other versions could be operated by hand, by animal, wind or water power. These machines were very popular as they were easy to build and repair and capable of drawing huge amounts of water. During the Song dynasty in 1074 AD there was a drought so severe, boats could not move up the canal; 42 dragon backbone pumps were set up to draw water from the Liang river in Wuxi. Five days later the canal boats were sailing again.

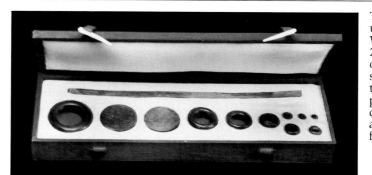

This set of weights was used in Chu, one of the Warring States of 475–221 BC. When the state of Qin conquered these states and unified China, the victorious Qin emperor established standard weights, measures and even axle widths for the whole country.

1   2

Dragon backbone water pumps operated by hand (1) or by treadmill (2) have been used for 2,300 years to irrigate rice. An endless wooden chain runs through a flume and around a pair of wheels. One wheel dips in the canal, the other hangs over the ditch beside the field above. Square boards called pallets, which are attached to the links, lift water up through the flume as the chain is turned.

A giant waterwheel is turned by the flowing river. As it revolves, sections of bamboo attached to the wheel's rim pick up water and lift it up to the flume where it is discharged. Invented 1,400 years ago, wheels like this have irrigated crops and pumped water for whole cities.

The *tong che* is a large, vertical, waterwheel with bamboo or wooden buckets attached to its rim. The lower edge of the wheel dips into the river and as it is turned by the current the buckets are filled, carried up high and discharged into a flume that runs into the irrigation ditch. The *tong che* may also be driven by animal power. It came into use in the 7th century AD. In his *Ode to a Waterwheel*, the Song dynasty poet Wang Ling wrote: "I am in use whenever there is a drought; what can you dragons do about it?" Dragons were supposed to control the rain so the farmer is saying that with the invention of the waterwheel he can irrigate his fields whether rain falls from the Heavens or not.

Ancient Grain Processing Machinery

Grain is processed in two stages. First it is hulled–beaten to loosen the indigestible bran–then ground in a mill to make flour. The water-powered tilt hammer was introduced in the 1st century AD during the Han dynasty. It was driven by a shaft which was rotated by a waterwheel. Cams fixed along the length of the shaft caused the hammers to rise and fall as it rotated. With the aid of this machine all the farmer had to do was pour the grain into the mortar so it could be beaten by the falling stone pestle of the trip hammer. All the hard work was done by water power.

Mills consist of pairs of flat stones with the upper stone rotating against the stone beneath it. Grain (millet, rice, soybean, wheat, barley, sorghum or corn) is poured in through a hole in the upper stone and the flour which results spills out through the gap between the two stones. The width of this gap determines whether the mill grinds coarse or fine. Mills may be driven by human, animal, wind or water power. In China, the latter was most readily available and water mills were built in which up to nine pairs of millstones might be driven through a geartrain by a single waterwheel.

Ancient Wheeled Transport

The wheel was known in China at least 3,600 years ago during the Shang dynasty when the kings went to battle riding two-wheeled chariots. During the Warring States Period (5th-3rd centuries BC) the wheelbarrow was invented, about 1,000

Windmills appeared in both China and the west about 800 years ago but the Chinese design has a vertical instead of a horizontal shaft. This means that its junk-like sails will turn regardless of the wind's direction. This windpump was used to draw brine from salt ponds on the coast near Tianjin.

Four water-driven hammers hull a farmer's rice. The invention of the waterwheel led to a host of water-driven machines: furnance-blowers, silk reeling machines, trip-hammers for forging metal and making paper pulp, mills for grinding wheat and millet.

years before it appeared in the west. The "nest cart" used for military spotting dates from the 8th-5th centuries BC. This was a mobile observation tower which could be hoisted up by means of a windlass, rather like a portable elevator. An observer could stand in the tower like a bird in a nest, so it was called a "nest cart". During the early part of the Han dynasty (2nd and 1st centuries BC) the four- and eight-wheeled carriages were invented. During the period of the Three Kingdoms which followed the Han in the 3rd century AD these were joined by the odometer wagon and the south-pointing carriage.

The odometer wagon was used for marking distances in units of *li* (0.5 km). The axle was fitted with a reduction gear train which drove a camshaft. The gearing ensured that for every *li* travelled the cam made one revolution and in doing so it raised the arms of wooden figures which beat a drum to mark the distance.

The south-pointing carriage was rather more complicated. It was a two-wheeled chariot with a complex gearing system connected to a vertical shaft supporting a pointing wooden figure of a man. A system of five transmission gears with ropes which could cause them to engage or disengage ensured that the figure always pointed south, no matter in which direction the carriage was travelling. This was the world's first example of an automatic engaging and disengaging gear system.

The odometer wagon and the south-pointing carriage were two of the vehicles in the train that accompanied the emperors in their tours of inspection, consequently they were always splendidly decorated.

The Earliest Seismograph

In 132 AD, Zhang Heng, an outstanding scientist of the later Han dynasty, invented the world's first detector of earthquakes. It consisted of a closed bronze urn with a ring of eight dragons facing out of its rim. Between the jaws of each dragon was a bronze ball and sitting around the base of the urn were eight bronze toads with their mouths open gaping up towards the dragons. In 138 AD Zhang Heng was hosting a meeting at his house when, suddenly, the ball in the mouth of the dragon on the west side of the seismograph fell into the mouth of the toad beneath it. At the sound of the

The winnowing fan which blows chaff off grain was used in China 1,300 years before it appeared in the west. Threshed grain goes into the hopper at the top and falls down through a blast of air from the fan. The chaff blows off and the heavier grain falls into the bin below. Similar fans were used to cool great houses by blowing air over blocks of ice. The Chinese wheelbarrow with its load over the wheel is very manoeuvrable. It dates from 230 BC–1,000 years before the western wheelbarrow.

The odometer wagon used gears which caused wooden figures to beat a drum each time it covered one *li* (about 0.5 km) in its ceremonial measurement of road lengths and land boundaries.

falling ball the visitors rushed to look but none had felt an earthquake. Many of them doubted that one had taken place and those who tended not to take science seriously ridiculed Zhang Heng. But a few days later a report came in by mail saying that there had been an earthquake in Long xi (now Gansu province) at the time and in the direction indicated by the seismograph. This revelation left Zhang Heng's critics tongue-tied and most embarrassed.

The seismograph worked on the principle of inertia. Inside the urn was a rod or pendulum. When the urn tilted in the direction of any tremor that shook it, the pendulum pressed on the jaws of the dragon facing the tremor, causing it to open its jaws and drop its ball into the mouth of the toad sitting below. Thus the clanging of the pendulum and the fall of the ball would indicate that an earthquake had taken place and also point the direction of its source.

The world's first detector of distant earthquakes, this bronze urn has eight dragons holding balls between their jaws. If the urn is tilted by an earth tremor, a pendulum tilts inside it and opens the jaws of the dragon facing the source of the tremor. The ball drops into the mouth of the frog sitting below. The clanging of the pendulum and the fall of the ball indicate the time and the direction of the earthquake. This seismograph was invented in 132 AD by Zhang Heng.

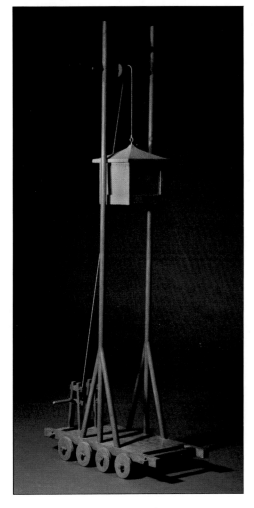

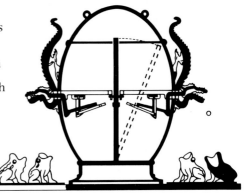

The "nest cart" was a mobile lookout platform used during the battles of the Spring and Autumn period more than 2,500 years ago. The spotting platform was like a ship's crow's nest which could be raised with a windlass to give a clear view of the battlefield. The cart could be drawn either by men or by horses wearing efficient breast-strap harness to make the best use of their strength. This was a problem that even the Romans failed to solve!

Bronze Casting

China's bronze age began about 4,000 years ago and lasted 2,000 years, leaving to posterity huge numbers of ritual objects, musical instruments, weapons, tools and household utensils. The mastery of materials and casting techniques, exquisitely intricate design and superb craftsmanship that characterize these objects have since become symbolic of the products of China's artists of all ages.

An outstanding example of the early period of bronze casting is the Si Mu Wu *ding* made during the Shang dynasty about 3,200 years ago. This ritual vessel is 1.33 m high, 1.66 m long, 0.79 m wide and weighs 875 kg–the largest bronze object ever found. Cast inside it are the three characters *Si Mu Wu* which means that the vessel was cast by the Shang king Wen Ding in honour of his mother. The casting of such a mammoth vessel was a multiple step process. The ceramic mould was assembled in pieces. Four large pieces sufficed for the sides of the vessel and another 24 were needed to cast the core, the legs, the bottom, the handles and the decoration. Six large furnaces 80 cm in diameter were needed to melt the huge amount of bronze needed. The molten metal was poured down troughs into the mould. The handles or "ears" were added later. Bronze smelting and casting of pieces as massive and complex as this were unknown in the west at this time.

In 1978 a set of bells was excavated from a tomb of the state of Chu dating back to the late Spring and Autumn period, 5th century BC. (At this time China was ruled by the Zhou king who delegated much of his authority to a number of feudal lords who each ruled small states such as Chu.) Musical instruments were very important in ancient rituals and bells most important of all. As symbols of the ruler's rank and authority they were played at the audiences of the king with his lords, at banquets and at religious and state ceremonies. This set of nine bells ranges in size from 21.6–11.7 cm long and 2.3–0.8 kg in mass. Each bell bears the same characters and decoration. On the inside there is a groove which adjusted the pitches of the principal and secondary tones of each bell after casting.

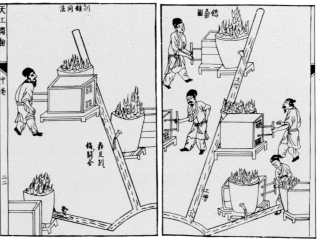

Bronze is melted in six furnaces raised to a great heat by double action piston bellows. Molten metal runs into the mould through clay channels. The double action piston bellows delivers air in a steady blast instead of a series of puffs. This produces the very high temperatures necessary.

Weapons 2,500–3,500 years old: a sword, a spearhead and a poleaxe (also shown wielded by the charioteer on the left) testify to the importance of bronze. Bronze casting in China began 4,000 years ago.

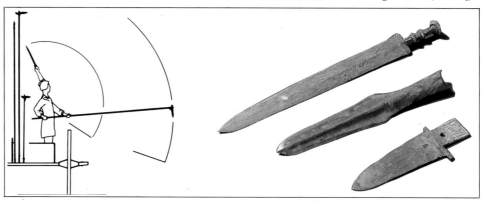

Animal- and bird-shaped jugs were filled with wine at the feasts of the kings of more than 3,000 years ago and bronze vessels were placed in their tombs. This 23-cm high elephant is covered with detail (note the animal crawling up its foreleg). This was made possible by the casting of bronze in fine ceramic moulds. The copper carbonate patina which covers the surface is now part of its beauty.

Huge bronze cauldrons were the most impressive objects placed in the tombs of the Shang aristocracy. This 38-cm high cauldron is unusual in being decorated with a starkly natural human face. Five mould sections with the decoration hollowed out formed the cauldron body around a central core, with about two dozen accessory moulds for the legs, handles and "ears."

Other ritual objects made during the bronze age included sacrificial vessels and wine jugs that were often cast in the form of animals and birds such as elephants or owls. Meanwhile the Chinese bronze workers were also turning out weapons: knives, spears, double-edged swords, halberds and dagger-axes that were carried on the ends of long poles.

Mining and Smelting the Copper of Verdigris Mountain

The superb craftsmanship of the bronze workers of the Shang and Zhou dynasties between the 16th and 8th centuries BC was backed up by a remarkable technology of mining and smelting. One of the greatest of the old mines was at Mt. Tonglu on the banks of the Yangtze in the hills that surround Daye lake. According to ancient records the area was rich in copper ore: "Every time it rained there was a patina like snowflakes or small beans which embellished the surface of the stones of the ground." The appearance of this "copper grass" which bloomed like jade orchids attracted generations of miners to Mt. Tonglu. Archaeological evidence for mining activity dates from the Spring and Autumn period of the Zhou dynasty (8th century BC) to the end of the Han dynasty (3rd century AD). During this period the mine shafts were pushed ever deeper from 10 to 50 m and widened from 60 x 60 cm to 80 x 80 cm. "Modern" techniques including the driving of vertical, sloping and blind shafts and the cutting of horizontal galleries were used to create an integrated network of tunnels and galleries. The works were supported by wooden frames with mortise and tenon joints either in an open frame with spaces between the props or in the form of a shed.

The early miners also had to tackle difficult problems of ventilation, drainage and lighting as well as the need to install rope and pulley systems for extracting the ore. Ventilation was achieved by placing the openings to the shafts at different levels to create a natural draught. Abandoned galleries were sealed off to ensure that air was forced into the deepest workings. The mine was drained by wooden troughs which led the water to pits at the bottoms of the shafts from which it could be hauled up and out of the mine by means of buckets. A parallel bucket and pulley system working in steps

Rows of trestles mark the course of a mine at Mt. Tonglu near Wuhan, south of the Yangtze. Copper was mined and smelted here for 1,000 years, from the 8th century BC to the 2nd century AD. This is a crosscut tunnel which connected the drifts where the ore was dug to the shafts that ran 50 m up to the surface. Also found were arrangements for drainage and ventilation, winding machinery, furnaces, moulds, iron and bronze tools and baskets for carrying the ore.

Windlasses were used to lift ore out of the Mt. Tonglu copper mine. Split bamboo baskets were used to haul the ore from the drifts to the bottoms of the shafts. This basket, still full of copper ore, was found exactly as it was left 2,000 years ago. Wooden buckets were also used, to remove water which drained into pits at the bottoms of the mineshafts.

was used to haul the copper ore up from shafts many metres deep.

Smelting of the ore was performed directly at Mt. Tonglu. After crushing, sifting and the addition of fluxing materials it was smelted in a vertical blast-furnace constructed of fire-resistant terracotta, quartzite, ironstone or kaolin ("China clay"). The furnace was about 1.5 m high, oval in shape with a hearth area of about 0.2 m². The furnace had a trumpet-shaped vent at the top and a metal tap on the side for extraction of the molten copper and slag. The furnace temperature could be raised to 1,300°C and yielded copper ingots of 93% purity with only 0.7% copper in the slag–remarkable

technological achievements at that time.

Bronze casting in China had its origins in the Xia dynasty before the 16th century BC. The first moulds were made of stone but they were difficult to make and often cracked at high temperatures, so they were replaced by clay moulds as soon as developments in ceramic technology permitted it. Clay moulds developed in complexity from single-faced to double-faced and to composite moulds that fitted together like a three-dimensional jigsaw puzzle. As far as possible even the most complex pieces were cast in one unit. Handles and decorations were sometimes cast-on later but only when one-piece casting was impossible.

Mass-production methods were also developed. Simple pieces needed in large quantities such as arrowheads or the knife-shaped currency of the Spring and Autumn and Warring States periods of the later Zhou dynasty were usually cast in large numbers by pouring bronze through a stack of inter-connecting moulds.

Another bronze-casting technique was the "lost-wax" process which is particularly useful for casting fine detail and small objects. In China this was developed by the Warring States period in the 5th century BC. First a wax model was made as a perfect image of the desired bronze object. This was then placed in a box and covered with

Purple flowers attracted miners to Mt. Tonglu. These are indicator plants which betray the copper in the soil by their special colour.

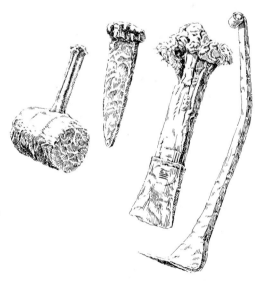

Wrought iron hammers, chisels and crowbars began to replace bronze tools around 600 BC. Iron was melted and cast 500 years later in China; 2,000 years later in the west.

RECONSTRUCTION OF MT. TONGLU SMELTING FURNACE

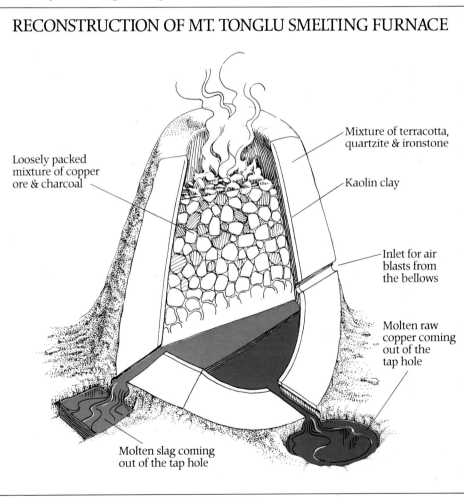

Mixture of terracotta, quartzite & ironstone

Kaolin clay

Loosely packed mixture of copper ore & charcoal

Inlet for air blasts from the bellows

Molten raw copper coming out of the tap hole

Molten slag coming out of the tap hole

Copper was smelted in blast furnaces lined with kaolin or "China clay." The crushed ore was mixed with charcoal and converted to metallic copper in a blast of air from a bellows. The heavy copper sank to the bottom where it flowed out through a tap hole while the lighter slag floated off through a higher tap. Tin was added later to make bronze. The kaolin which lined these furnaces could withstand the temperatures of well over 1,000°C developed by a forced draught. This allowed the melting of copper, bronze and iron in large quantities–a process the west found difficult. "China clay" was also an essential ingredient of another product, porcelain.

several layers of clay. When this had dried it was fired, hardening the clay to a ceramic and melting out the original wax model, leaving a perfect mould. Bronze was poured into the space left by the "lost wax" model. When the bronze had cooled the clay mould was broken away, revealing a casting that was shaped exactly like the wax original.

The splendid bronze lions, elephants, cranes and fabulous beasts of the old Imperial Palace (now the Palace Museum) and Summer Palace in Beijing were cast by the lost wax process, a technique that is still used in modern industry.

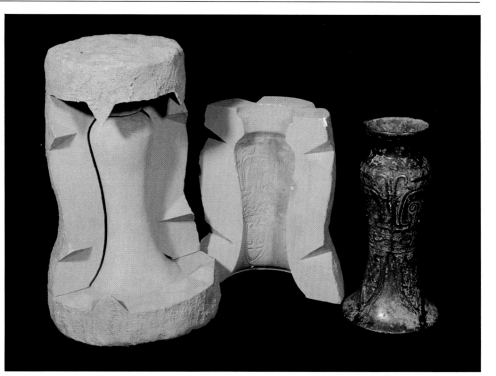

This 3,000-year-old bronze goblet was originally fashioned in clay and a removable multi-piece mould made of it. Then the original was ground down to the desired thickness of the final cup. The mould was replaced and molten bronze was poured into the space between mould and core.

This massive bronze lion in the former Imperial Palace in Beijing was made by the "lost wax" process at the time of the European Renaissance. Imagine the scale of the project and the amount of bronze required for this casting.

When the bronze inside a stack mould cools, the mould is broken to release the castings. These are broken off the connecting bronze stalk.

Arrows were mass-produced 3,500 years ago by pouring bronze into a compound mould. The impressions of the arrowheads were joined by grooves which ensured that the bronze would flow smoothly through the mould. This clay mould dates back to the Shang dynasty of 3,100 –3,600 years ago. The castings emerge from the moulds attached to one another by the stalks which form in the connecting channels. These stalks of waste metal are known as "sprue." Similar moulds were used for articles such as buckles and harness fittings which were also needed in large quantities.

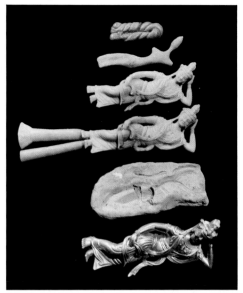

The "lost wax" process is used to cast a figure of a dancer dressed in the style of the Tang dynasty, 1,200 years ago. Wax is moulded around a clay core and the figure is then sculpted to look exactly like the desired object. Pins are inserted to hold the core in place and wax rods are added to provide pouring channels for the bronze. The figure and rods are covered with clay and baked in a kiln. As the clay hardens, the wax melts out, creating a hollow, hard, ceramic mould with a clay core. Molten bronze is poured in to replace the "lost wax." When the metal has cooled, the mould is broken to reveal an exact replica in bronze of the wax original.

Bronze casting continues to be an important skill in modern China. This man is ready to pour bronze which has been melted by burning charcoal, with a draught supplied by an electric blower rather than a double-piston bellows. But the principles remain the same. Today, there is a steady demand for reproductions of the great bronzes of more than 3,000 years ago while many of the techniques that go into making them are also put to use in modern industry.

Medicine and Health

As early as the Spring and Autumn and Warring States Periods (770-221 BC) the *Yellow Emperor's Classic of Internal Medicine* the theoretical foundations of Chinese medicine. Through several thousand years of struggle against disease, the Chinese people have established a unique set of theories of medical treatment and prevention.

From prehistory comes the legend of the "sage king," Shen Nong, who lived more than 5,000 years ago and is supposed to have "tasted 100 kinds of medicinal herbs." By 221 BC, a great variety of records concerning herbal medicines had accumulated but *Shen Nong's Classic on Herbs,* completed during the late Han dynasty (2nd century AD), is the oldest Chinese pharmacological work extant. It lists 365 different kinds of herbal medicine divided into three grades of quality with their places of production, methods of collection, preparation, prescriptions, medical uses and compatibility with each other all described.

Li Shizhen (1518-1593 AD), a pharmacologist of the Ming dynasty, travelled through more than half of China and suffered all kinds of hardships before compiling his great pharmacological work *Compendium of Materia Medica* which took him 27 years to complete. In this work, Li Shizhen summarized China's medical achievements prior to his time, listing 1,892 different herbs and 11,000 prescriptions. In his redrawing of the medicinal herbs, he corrected previous mistakes and classified the herbs scientifically according to their natural attributes. This was a great contribution to the world's knowledge of pharmacology, mineralogy, botany and zoology.

The theories of Chinese pharmacology are derived from the natural attributes of herbs and their ability to cure the malfunctions of the human body. These theories hold that different diseases must be treated according to the special attributes of the medicinal herbs: "Four Spirits," "Five Tastes," "Floating or Sinking," "Rising and Lowering." The "Four Spirits" in drugs are the body's response to a particular medicine: cold, hot, warm or cool. The "Five Tastes" are sour,

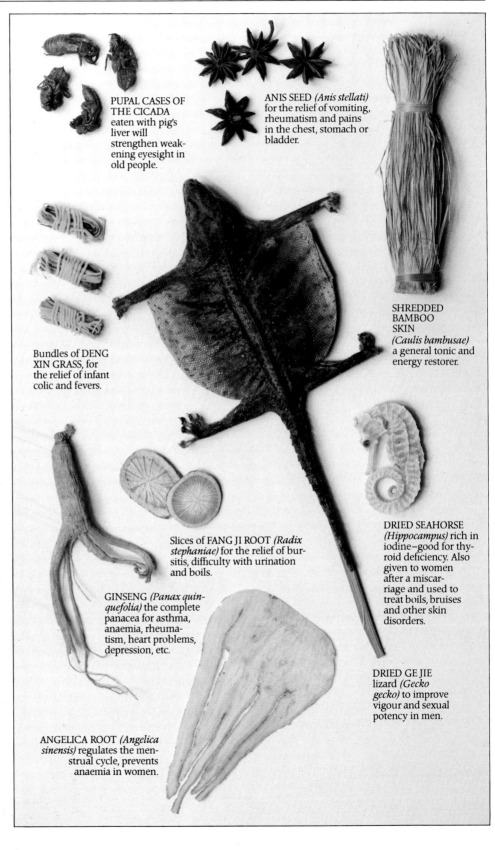

PUPAL CASES OF THE CICADA eaten with pig's liver will strengthen weakening eyesight in old people.

ANIS SEED *(Anis stellati)* for the relief of vomiting, rheumatism and pains in the chest, stomach or bladder.

SHREDDED BAMBOO SKIN *(Caulis bambusae)* a general tonic and energy restorer.

Bundles of DENG XIN GRASS, for the relief of infant colic and fevers.

Slices of FANG JI ROOT *(Radix stephaniae)* for the relief of bursitis, difficulty with urination and boils.

GINSENG *(Panax quinquefolia)* the complete panacea for asthma, anaemia, rheumatism, heart problems, depression, etc.

DRIED SEAHORSE *(Hippocampus)* rich in iodine—good for thyroid deficiency. Also given to women after a miscarriage and used to treat boils, bruises and other skin disorders.

DRIED GE JIE lizard *(Gecko gecko)* to improve vigour and sexual potency in men.

ANGELICA ROOT *(Angelica sinensis)* regulates the menstrual cycle, prevents anaemia in women.

bitter, hot, sweet, salty, with each taste related to a different function. To meet different medical needs, the Chinese doctor was armed with more than 5,000 different kinds of herbal drugs in which the basic ingredients might be given as pills, powders, pastes, tonics or tea-like decoctions.

Diagnosis in Chinese medicine depends upon making an overall analysis of the illness and of the patient's condition. Every symptom has to be investigated. This is done through the "Four Examinations": inspection, smelling, questioning, and taking the pulses. Inspection discloses the patient's mental state as revealed by his complexion, facial expression, gestures and general behaviour. The condition of the tongue is also believed to be important. If it has a yellow coating it means that "fire" has risen in the stomach, causing poor digestion and loss of appetite. If the tongue is red or purple it could mean that the heart is not pumping sufficient blood. The odours given off when the patient talks, breathes or coughs and the smell of his excreta reveal the inner condition of his body.

Questioning is important in both Chinese and Western medicine. The patient is asked about his daily life, his associates and his environment, what he feels might be the cause of his illness and how he has been treated so far.

Taking the pulse is of especial importance in Chinese medicine and this is a far more elaborate procedure than in the west. The doctor feels the radial artery in the patient's wrist. This was thought to be one of the junction points of the arteries of the body which could reveal the functioning of the *qi,* the "vital energy" and the state of the blood within the human body. The conditions of the pulses felt for by the fingers included their depth, location, speed, power and rhythm. Pulse conditions may be divided into "floating, sinking, slow, frequent, smooth, uneven, taut, thready, strong, weak," etc. The *Diagnostic Handbook* written by Shi Fa during the Song dynasty in 1241 AD included 33 diagrams illustrating pulse conditions which may be compared to modern electrocardiograms–the former describe the changing waves of a pulsebeat, the latter the changing waveform of a heartbeat.

A "floating pulse" is one that can be felt when lightly pressed with the fingers. If

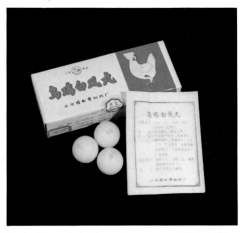

Dark-skinned chickens are processed into pills for the regulation of menstruation. Chinese *materia medica* often seem strange to people from the west, especially those who have forgotten the origins of some of our own drugs: penicillin from mould, quinine and aspirin from tree barks, insulin from calf pancreas. Today, Chinese medicines are being subjected to careful analysis in both east and west to find out exactly how they work.

The Universal Medicine Shop in Beijing, founded by the Le family in the mid-17th century, is still run by their descendants. Chests, like this revolving cabinet (below) from the Imperial clinic, contain thousands of plant, animal and mineral ingredients from all parts of China. These are blended to fill prescriptions for treatments that may be thousands of years old.

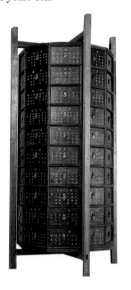

This Boshan (Mt. Bo) incense burner was cast during the former Han dynasty, 206 BC– 8 AD. Through their interest in alchemy the Chinese learned that burning sulphur or the dried flowers of chrysanthemums would destroy insect pests. Incense was also burned in temples and homes to create a pleasant aroma.

the fingers press harder the pulse becomes weaker, showing that the disease is on the surface of the body where the conflict between the organism and the "exterior evil" causing the disease is taking place. An example would be the beginning of a cold.

A "sinking pulse" can be felt only when the fingers press hard. This shows that the disease is deep within the body and caused by a deficiency of the vital *yang* force. This is commonly observed in cases of heart disease.

A "smooth pulse," when pressed, "moves like the rolling of pearls." This is a common symptom of asthma due to excessive phlegm, storing up of blood and fever.

An "uneven pulse moves bumping to and fro and is often held up." It is a symptom of the heart condition angina pectoris in which the arteries do not expand sufficiently to permit the additional bloodflow to the heart which is necessary during physical exertion.

Accurate diagnosis based on the Four Examinations of questioning, inspection, smelling and taking the pulses requires much practice and experience before a doctor can make a comprehensive analysis according to the theories of traditional Chinese medicine.

Acupuncture and moxibustion are both unique to Chinese medicine and were invented in ancient times. Neither of these treatments involves the taking of drugs. Needles are implanted in certain points of the patient's body or a bar of moxa (dried mugwort tinder) is burnt over these same spots. These two treatments are commonly used together. They are easy to give and may be applied to a wide range of diseases as well as being used to relieve pain during surgery and in the treatment of gynaecological, paediatric and ear, nose and throat problems.

The *Historical Records* compiled by the historian Sima Qian in the Han dynasty (2nd century BC) include the story of a famous doctor of the Warring States Period (475–221 BC) called Bian Que.

"One day when Bian Que arrived in the State of Guo he found the whole state preparing for the funeral of the prince who had been dead for half a day. Judging from the information the people could give him, Bian Que felt it unlikely

This 2,000-year-old exercise chart with over forty different movements was found in a Han dynasty tomb at Mawangdui. China recognized early on the value of breath control exercises–such as *Tai Ji*–in curing illness and prolonging life.

Moxibustion is applied by a doctor to a patient who has to be held down by his attendants.
Cones or bars of smouldering mugwort tinder are applied to the acupuncture points on the skin. It is a painful process that leaves scars but it is supposed to relieve skin diseases, insomnia, local paralysis, toothache and convulsions. It has even been tried against rabies. Moxibustion has been practised for 3,000 years and is still popular today.

These instruments were used in throat operations 100 years ago. As in the west, surgery was discouraged in ancient China because of religious disapproval of interference with the body. Nevertheless, by the 2nd century AD operations were being performed on the chest, intestines, ovary, nose, skull and bladder. This was helped by acupuncture and possibly by using opium and cannabis as analgesics more than 1,000 years before the invention of surgical anaesthesia in North America.

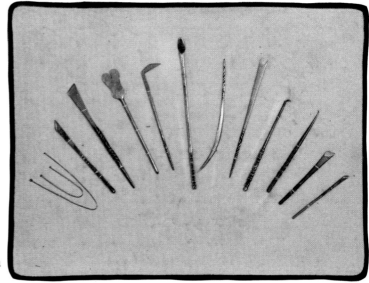

that the prince's symptoms would have caused him to die. He asked to enter the palace to take a look. Inside the palace, Bian Que only had to touch the prince's wrists and thighs to conclude that he was not really dead. By applying acupuncture and moxibustion together with certain drugs he gave emergency treatment to the prince who soon came back to life. After this Bian Que was honoured as the famous doctor who could bring the dead back to life!"

This story shows that acupuncture and moxibustion have been important medical treatments in China for more than 2,000 years.

According to Chinese medicine, the human body is a small world to which man must adapt himself. This theory of "agreement between man and nature" holds that the human body must follow the natural law of birth in the spring, growth in the summer, harvest in autumn, storage in winter. Only by doing thus can human beings enjoy health. Since ancient times, traditional Chinese medicine has maintained the concept of active prevention with the saying, "The superb workman gives treatment before the patient falls ill." This means that an excellent doctor will strive to prevent illness and preserve the health of the people.

The way to achieve this is to keep the body in a constantly active state. According to legend there was once a man in ancient China by name of Peng Zu who lived more than 800 years. He achieved this by deliberately controlling his breath, giving out the old and taking in the new. He also exercised his body in imitation of the birds and beasts, thus prolonging his life. During the period of the Three Kingdoms (220-280 AD) the famous doctor Hua Tuo devised the *Five Animal Exercises* in imitation of the movements of the tiger, deer, ape, bear and crane. These exercises helped cure and prevent disease. Hua Tuo and his pupil Wu Pu and others among his followers lived more than 90 years. Later, the *Five Animal Exercises* and the deep breathing exercises were developed into the *Ba Duan Jin* and *Tai Ji* exercises that continue to strengthen and keep healthy the bodies of millions of Chinese and practitioners in the west to this day.

Acupuncture is shown in the upper panel of this 1,900-year-old tombstone.

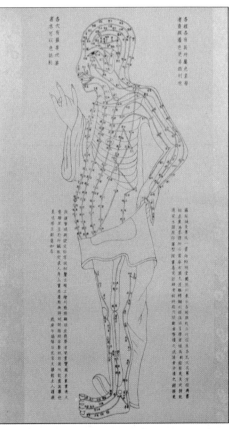

An acupuncture chart shows the acupoints connected by acutracts. The effectiveness of acupuncture cannot be doubted. Research on animals by Bruce Pomeranz of the University of Toronto shows that acupuncture stimulates the release of endorphin–the brain's natural painkiller.

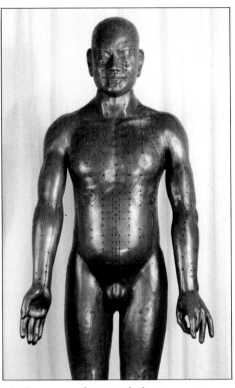

A hollow copper figure with the acupuncture points left as tiny holes was used for medical training. The figure was covered with wax, then filled with water which trickled out whenever a student hit the right spot with his needle. This figure is 700–1,000 years old.

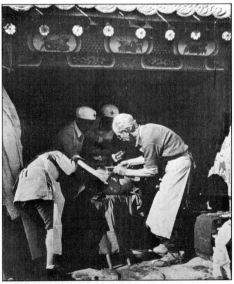

Adopting the maxim, "Doctors: go to the wounded; don't wait for the wounded to come to you," Dr. Norman Bethune left Canada to help the Chinese in 1938. He died caring for the wounded in 1939. His selflessness has made him a hero in China.

Ceramics

The ability to make ceramic pottery is an almost universal mark of a culture that has taken the first steps in its transformation into a true civilization. Before the discovery of pottery and bronze the only containers available to mankind were those provided by nature, such as shells, gourds or pipes of bamboo. China has led the world in this branch of technology almost from the beginning and when the fine, delicate porcelain now called "china" reached the west it was to have almost as much impact on society as China's other great inventions, paper and printing, gunpowder and the compass.

Archaeologists have found that the Chinese people who lived in scattered villages in the Yellow River basin and along the sea coast 8,000 years ago were makers of pottery. It is thought that they may have discovered it when baskets they had waterproofed with clay were accidentally burned and hardened. This led to the deliberate shaping of clay pots which were first dried in the shade then baked in the fire. The kiln for firing pottery was known at least 6,500 years ago but the wheel which allowed pots to be turned out faster, with thinner walls and with much more elegance did not appear until about 5,000 years ago.

In 1921, archaeologists excavated a neolithic village at Yangshao in Henan Province. Among the finds were reddish-brown pottery decorated with sand or stamped with geometric designs dating back 5,000 years. These finds were the first representatives found of what is now known as the "Yangshao Culture." In 1928, another site belonging to the patriarchal society of the late neolithic of 4,000 years ago was excavated at Longshan in Shandong Province. This has since become known as the "Longshan Culture." Its pottery shows considerable advances over that of Yangshao. The colours and designs were far more varied: red, grey, black, white, variegated, with blue-green sand decoration, stamp-designed, thin shell or openwork like a basket. More importantly, Longshan pottery, unlike that of Yangshao, was thrown on a wheel, not built up by hand.

More important than the wheel was the Chinese expertise in building high-temperature kilns, which eventually led to the dis-

This earthenware burial jar was placed in a tomb more than 5,000 years ago by people of the neolithic "Yangshao" culture in Zhejiang province. It is built up of red clay, not thrown on the potter's wheel which was invented about 2,000 years later. It was decorated with mineral pigments brushed on before firing.

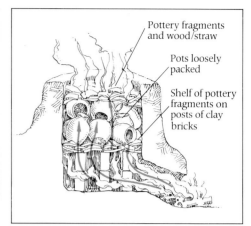

The kilns of 5,000 years ago were dug out of earthen banks and lined with clay. The pots were stacked over firebricks and covered with pottery fragments and matted branches. The aim of all kilns is a prolonged, high, steady temperature. The Chinese pre-eminence in ceramics was due to their possession of excellent clay and to their genius in using it not only for making pottery but for the lining of their kilns which were to become the hottest in the world. Simple kilns like this were found in the excavation of Ban Po village, a 5,000-year-old settlement.

More than 7,000 individually fashioned, life-size, terracotta figures of warriors, horses and ministers were buried to guard the body of the first Emperor of Qin, who died in 209 BC. The terracotta army took the place of real soldiers who usually accompanied their emperor to his grave. The entrance to the tomb was filled in and guarded by automatic crossbows but this did not deter the tomb robbers who pilfered the body and stripped it of its jewellery centuries ago. This mighty army remains, a suitable reminder of the emperor who conquered the "Warring States" to reunify China and then ordered the completion of the Great Wall which was finished in 214 BC.

covery of porcelain. This was a long, slow process. About 3,000 years ago, during the time of the slave-based Shang dynasty, workers discovered that superior pottery could be made with white clay from the Gaoling (Kaolin) hills of Jiangxi Province. Later they discovered that those pieces that were placed in the hottest section of the kiln emerged harder and of a better quality than those that were baked in the cooler sections. Finally it was discovered that coating the surface of the clay with silicate glaze prior to firing would give it a clean, brilliant, non-porous finish. The result of these three developments: high temperature kilns, kaolin clay and silicate glaze was blue-green glazeware. This was the earliest form of celadon.

Between the 11th century BC and the 3rd century AD–the Zhou, Qin and Han dynasties, white and coloured glazed pottery continued to develop. The basic kaolin was improved by addition of quartz and felspar and kiln temperatures of more than 1,000°C, making the final product harder, finer and more translucent–closer to modern porcelain. Glazes were produced in more colours: green, pale green, brownish yellow and chestnut brown.

Pottery was no longer a material suitable only for making household utensils but a substance equally suited in its wide variety to the manufacture of bricks, tiles or works of art. Bricks were first made about 2,200 years ago during the Qin dynasty (221-206BC). When the first Qin emperor died in 209BC his tomb was packed with a mighty army of 7,000 lifesize terracotta figures of horses, warriors and ministers, beautifully fashioned. During the Han dynasty, which followed the Qin (206 BC-220 AD), the heavy, glazed tiles which became so characteristic of Chinese buildings were developed and people were buried, not with the massive terracotta figures of Qin times, but with more delicate celadon models of houses, farms and figurines. Since the timber buildings of 2,000 years ago have long since perished, these tomb models of the Han dynasty provide us with the richest source of information we now have of the architecture and living styles of that time.

The period from the 3rd to 10th centuries AD saw the maturation of Chinese ceramic technology. This is the period of the "three-coloured (green, yellow, cream) Tang ware."

Earthenware models of houses, people, and animals were placed in the tombs of the former Han dynasty, 206 BC-28 AD. By this time glazes had been discovered, making pottery clean and waterproof. Models like this little manor house are reminders of the times when great men were buried with servants, concubines and horses. They also show how the Chinese lived 2,000 years ago, now that all the buildings of that time have disappeared.

Clay moulds, like this beast head of the Warring States period, 475–221 BC, were made for the mass production of ceramic sculptures. They were similar to the ceramic piece-moulds used for bronze-casting from about 1300 BC onwards.

This celadon jug in the form of a sheep was made under the Eastern Jin dynasty, 317–420 AD. Celadon is a ceramic finer than earthenware. Made out of kaolin ("China clay") fired at a high temperature, it was an important precursor of true porcelain. By this time, bronze casting had long declined from the predomin- ance it had enjoyed 1,000 years earlier and had been largely supplanted by ceramics. This jug is highly reminiscent of the animal-shaped wine vessels of the bronze age. It even has a green glaze similar in colour to the patina of old bronze.

These three colours were later joined by blue and eggplant, as seen in the famous horses and camels buried in the tombs of that time. Yixing in Jiangsu province was established as a pottery centre, achieving an international reputation which it still enjoys today. According to folklore, tea steeped in purple sand pottery from Yixing will keep its flavour even on the hottest summer days and the roots of any plant potted in it will never rot.

The first true porcelain, derived from the celadon of the Shang and Zhou dynasties, appeared during the 3rd-5th centuries AD, during the period of the Three Kingdoms and the Western and Eastern Jin dynasties. Later came white-and black-glazed porcelains.

From the 6th-10th centuries, during the Sui and Tang dynasties, the two kilns most representative of the factories of north and south China were the Xing potteries which produced white porcelain in the northern province of Hebei and the Yue kilns which produced celadon in the southern province of Zhejiang. The quality of their products was so fine, they were compared with snow and jade respectively. Lines from a classical poem praise the celadon of the time: "When the Yue kilns are opened in the wet winds of autumn, They take unto themselves the emerald hue of a thousand hills." White porcelain from Jingdezhen was known as "artificial jade."

In the 10th century, towards the end of the shortlived Five Dynasties period which followed the Tang, Chai Rong, also known as the Emperor Shi Zong of the Later Zhou dynasty, was a great connoisseur of porcelain and ordered the establishment of the Imperial kilns in Henan Province to turn out celadon which was praised as being "Like the blue sky following a rain," and as having "the blueness of the sky, the brightness of a mirror, the thinness of paper and the resonance of a chime-stone."

From the 10th-19th centuries porcelain was at its peak in moulding qualities, glazing materials, firing and quality and variety of painting and glazing. China had an unprecedented number of kilns and potters. It was written of Jingdezhen in Jiangxi province that the "craftsmen population could be counted in the hundreds of thousands." By now potting had become a sophisticated industry with an elaborate division of labour

This celadon jug for water or wine was made during the Tang dynasty. It was beautifully turned on the potter's wheel then fitted with a pair of bird-head handles. By this time, 618–907 AD, ceramics were becoming a true art form, fit for the patronage of emperors.

This three-colour, glazed earthenware figure of a *lokapala,* an armoured warrior with a phoenix-crowned helmet, served as a Buddhist tomb-guardian in the Tang dynasty, 8th century AD.

Ceramic moulds, similar to those used in bronze casting, were used to mass-produce these figures of dancing women during the Tang dynasty, 618–907 AD. The arms and bodies were moulded separately then stuck together with clay prior to firing. Singing girls, dancers and female musicians were popular in China from the earliest times. Clearly, the love of miniature figurines is also of great antiquity.

into firemen (who kept the kilns up to temperature), mixers (who prepared the glazes), workmen in clay, painters, etc.

Different kilns had their specialities. For example, the Ding kilns in Hebei and the Yaozhou kilns in Shaanxi were noted for their "jade-white," "sugar-white" and "ivory-white" procelains.

During the Song dynasty (10th-13th centuries) the two Zhang brothers operated kilns in Longquan County, Zhejiang province. The elder brother's kiln produced celadon that was unique for the irregular but even crackling of its surface. From the younger brother's kiln came light, greenish-blue celadon, the warm and delicate appearance of which beautifully complemented the elder brother's crackleware. The greatest developments in porcelain during this period were in colours and glazes. Traditionally, patterns had been incised or imprinted on the body of a piece before glazing or firing. This was called underglaze decoration. The blue and white porcelain so famous throughout China and abroad was produced in this manner, beginning in the Song dynasty in the 10th-13th centuries and flourishing through the Yuan and Ming dynasties to the 17th century. "Five Colours" (green, yellow, eggplant, red and blue) and "Contesting Colours," in which the five colours were outlined with blue, were developments of the Ming dynasty (14th-17th centuries). In "Contesting Colours" the blue outline was first painted under the glaze. The remaining colours were then applied as enamels requiring a second firing. The final development in this process was "Famille Rose," created in the Qing dynasty (17th-20th centuries). Red lead powder was mixed into the pigment and applied to the baked porcelain to create contrasts in colour intensity, light and dark shades and a soft lustre. The play of light and shadow on the surface of the porcelain gives a three-dimensional effect.

Jingdezhen in Jiangxi province is the capital of Chinese porcelain manufacture. At the time of the Former Han dynasty, 2,000 years ago, Jingdezhen was producing pottery and porcelain kilns were built there in the 6th century AD, during the Southern Chen dynasty. In the 10th century, during the Tang and the Five Dynasties, these kilns produced "artificial jade"–white porcelain. In the 11th century, one of the early Song

Ceramic pillows have a long history in China. This pillow is in the form of a prostrate tiger. Two birds, one perched on a rock, decorate the flat surface of the head-rest, an ideal spot for painting. The decoration was painted with iron oxide, then glazed prior to firing. Ceramic pillows were especially popular in north China during the Song dynasty. This pillow was made in Cizhou stoneware in the 12th century AD.

A boy riding a duck forms this 12th century pitcher. The duck's beak is the spout and the boy's sleeve the handle. Ducks and boys were popular themes in Song dynasty art, suggesting married bliss and many children. Perfectly white porcelain like this Dingware was sought for centuries. It was achieved by firing white kaolin mixed with felspar in kilns hotter than 1,100°C and firing again with a clear silicate glaze to create a hard, glassy finish.

The floral decoration on this Yaozhou ware bowl of the Song dynasty, 11th–12th centuries AD, was achieved by incision. The green celadon glaze is darker where it has collected in the furrows, creating an effect of subdued elegance for which Song dynasty art is famous.

Blue and white porcelain, like this Ming dynasty fruit dish with lotus decoration, first appeared at the end of the Song dynasty in the 13th century and reached its finest form in the Ming, 1368–1644 AD. The blue pigment was cobalt blue imported from Iran. Blue and white porcelain was exported in huge quantities to India, Arabia, Europe and even East Africa where fragments of it are found on the beaches to this day.

Emperors established an Imperial kiln at Jingdezhen to produce utilitarian and artistic porcelains for use in his own household and in those of the nobility. As this happened during the *Jing De* reign period, one of the five periods of the Emperor Zhen Zong's 25-year reign, the name of the porcelain city was changed from Changnanzhen to Jingdezhen. To this day, this ancient centre remains one of the most important pottery and porcelain making cities in China. It has produced the famous white porcelains of the Song, the underglaze red, and the blue and white of the Yuan, the "Contesting Colours" and "Five Colours" of the Ming and "Famille Rose" of the Qing–altogether more than 3,000 varieties, all of them rare and valuable.

A great range of glazes was produced at Jingdezhen: Jun red, Lang kiln red, rose, green, yellow, blue, black. All of these were fired in a reducing flame (i.e. the oxygen supply to the kiln was restricted), which made the colours more vivid and this gave them a very high quality.

Jingdezhen was a thriving market city by the time of the Ming. It was described as: "The place to which craftsmen come from the four corners of China and from which manufactures pour out to every part of the world." A poem describes the porcelain industry of Jingdezhen:

"Rows of tight-pressed pottery sheds open to the shore;
Ships come daily, their sails spread over the river;
As of old, workmen cherish their heaven-endowed skills;
Their wares could fill the coffers of the nation."

The ancestors of the modern Chinese, by their own industry and diligence created the first utilitarian objects in human history to be manufactured from a man-made material–earthenware. After thousands of years of constant work and painstaking study, ceramic artisans made their "ceramic garden bloom with a hundred flowers," presenting the beholder with all the beauty and variety of richly-made brocade. With the development of contacts between China and the world, ceramics were exported overland by the "Silk Road" that straddled Asia or went by the southeasterly

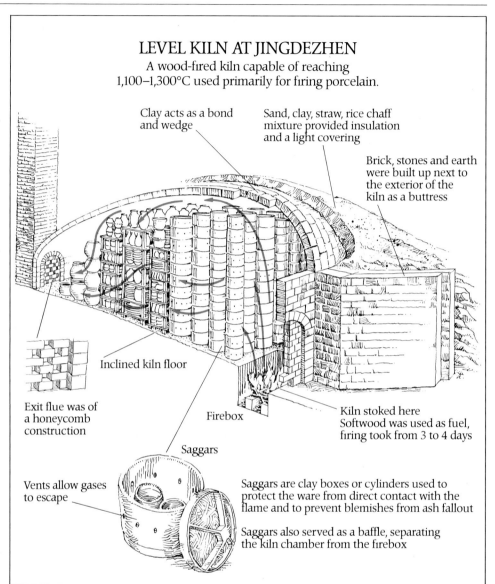

LEVEL KILN AT JINGDEZHEN
A wood-fired kiln capable of reaching 1,100–1,300°C used primarily for firing porcelain.

Clay acts as a bond and wedge

Sand, clay, straw, rice chaff mixture provided insulation and a light covering

Brick, stones and earth were built up next to the exterior of the kiln as a buttress

Inclined kiln floor

Exit flue was of a honeycomb construction

Firebox

Kiln stoked here
Softwood was used as fuel, firing took from 3 to 4 days

Saggars

Vents allow gases to escape

Saggars are clay boxes or cylinders used to protect the ware from direct contact with the flame and to prevent blemishes from ash fallout

Saggars also served as a baffle, separating the kiln chamber from the firebox

The secret of fine ceramics lies in kaolin ("China clay") and in kilns like this that are capable of the sustained 1,300°C needed to fuse it to form porcelain.

This crackleware bowl dates from 1821–1850 AD but the process for making it by careful rapid cooling after glazing was discovered 800 years earlier. Throughout most of that 800 years, before "china" became a household word, the west made do with coarse, unglazed, unhygienic terracotta earthenware.

sea route to be sold in the distant countries of Asia, Africa and Europe.

With advances in transport by sea, a single cargo of Chinese porcelain could number hundreds of thousands of pieces. Chinese ceramics have been the prized possessions of kings and aristocrats in many countries; Chinese celadon and porcelain have been exported to every corner of the globe. Chinese ceramics carry with them the deep friendship of the Chinese people – a friendship that will bloom forever!

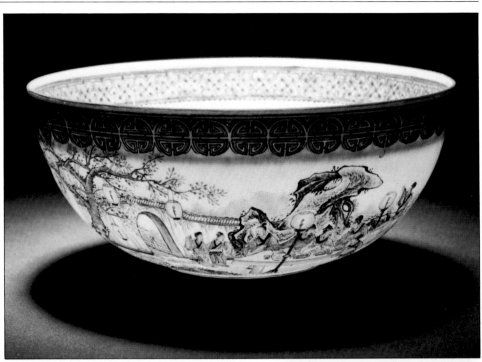

The eggshell thinness of this 1911 porcelain bowl was achieved by paring down the body on a lathe. Some pieces of eggshell porcelain are so thin that the rims appear to consist only of glaze. The delicacy of this bowl illustrates one of the many features of porcelain. Ceramic glazes and porcelain in their numerous applications–from sewage pipes to dinner ware–have revolutionized the lives of all people.

The "soufflé," or powder blue glaze on this porcelain bottle, was achieved by spraying the powdered cobalt pigment through a bamboo pipe prior to dipping it in the colourless glaze. Even colours were made by mixing the pigment into the glaze. This bottle was made during the great Kangxi period (1662-1722 AD) of the Qing dynasty, the time of Louis XIV of France, almost the exact contemporary of Emperor Kangxi.

Using a fine-pointed chisel-knife, a porcelain sculptor creates a delicate lattice out of a square of clay before it is put in the kiln for firing. Behind him are moulded busts in the Buddhist style of 1,200 years ago and a delicate basket of carved roses. These are just a few examples of the great versatility of porcelain which was perfected 1,500 years ago, 8,000 years after the beginnings of the Chinese ceramics industry.

Porcelain is still made in the former Imperial potteries. This "banana" vase, glazed in alternations of peach and crabapple *meirenzui* glaze, comes from Jingdezhen, which has been a ceramics centre for 2,000 years. Formerly Changnanzhen, its name changed in the 11th century in honour of the *Jing De* reign of the Emperor Zhen Zong who established a pottery there.

Silk Weaving

In ancient China the people spun and wove hemp, cotton and wool but the most prestigious textiles were made of silk. Long before direct contact was made with the west, China was known to Europe through trade along the trans-Asian Silk Road as "Seres," the "Silk Country."

The earliest evidence of weaving dates back six or seven thousand years ago to the neolithic period when people wove cloth from hemp and bean fibre. We know this from their habit of decorating pottery, such as that found at the Banpo site near Xi'an, with the impressions of hemp cloth and spinning whorls. Traces of 6,000-year-old cloth woven from hemp fibre and a remnant of hemp cloth about 4,000 years old with its woof and warp fibres in a ratio of 15 x 20 cm² were found in a cliff tomb in Wuyishan, Fujian province. By this time, textiles were playing an important role in the Chinese economy. During the Western Zhou period (11th to 8th centuries BC) a special bureau was established to supervise the production of hemp and to tax the hemp and beans that provided the textile fibres. At the same time, silk and wool were becoming more important.

The filament of the cocoon of the silkworm was first used for making textiles in China. This happened so long ago that the story of the origin of silk is buried in legend. Around 2600 BC the clan of the Yellow Emperor defeated the Jiu Li clan. Just as the Yellow Emperor and his followers were about to celebrate their victory, a beautiful maiden descended from the sky, cloaked in a horse pelt. In her hands she carried two skeins of silk, shimmering and shining, one gold and one silver. She presented the silk to the Yellow Emperor who ordered his people to weave cloth from it. When it was finished, the silk cloth resembled the clouds of the sky and the flowing waters of a mountain stream and was incomparably soft and beautiful. Form this gift of the goddess of silkworms, Matouniang, grew China's silk industry.

The oldest piece of silk yet found was excavated by archaeologists in 1958 at a neolithic site in Zhejiang province. A quantity of woven silk had been packed inside a bamboo container and buried about 4,700 years ago. The importance of the silk indus-

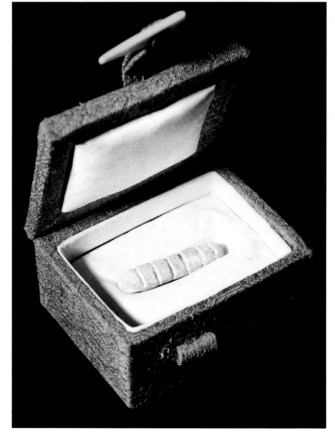

Weaving women sit in a circle working backstrap looms (found worldwide as the earliest of weaving devices) while their mistress is offered food by her servants. These figures, decorate a bronze lid which once covered a cowrie chest 75 cm in diameter. It was made by the Dian people of Yunnan, south-west China, 4,000–5,000 years ago.

A silkworm carved in jade testifies to the importance of silk, which dates back in legend to the beginnings of Chinese civilization. This silkworm, only 1.5 cm long, was found in a tomb mound in Anyang, ancient capital of the Shang dynasty (16th–11th centuries BC). Only the most valuable objects were placed in these tombs to be available in the afterlife.

try from the earliest times is also proven by the jade silkworms that were placed in the tombs of the slave-owning aristocracy of the Shang dynasty in the 16th-11th century BC. Traces of silk cloth have also been found on pieces of bronze and blades of jade buried in the tombs of the Shang period. One of these, preserved in the Palace Museum in Beijing, has a thundercloud pattern woven into it, indicating the growing sophistication of weaving techniques at that time.

Silk is woven into simple cloth, satin, damask, muslin, gauze, velvet, tapestry and brocade. Of these, brocade is the most complicated and so precious that the Chinese word for it is derived from the two characters *jin* (gold) and *bo* (silk) meaning that silk brocade and gold are of equal value. Silk brocade first appeared during the Western Zhou period in the 11th century BC. It evolved in three stages: (1) tabby–patterns based on the warp, (2) twill–patterns based on the woof, and (3) patterns which are combinations of tabby and twill. Representative of these three stages are: (1) a brown brocade with rectangular pattern excavated from a tomb of the Warring State of Chu near Changsha and about 2,300 years old; (2) a brocade with pulled nap excavated from the tomb at Mawangdui of a Han marchioness buried in 205 BC, also near Changsha in Hunan province; and (3) a brocade with peacock pattern excavated from a tomb at Asitana, Xinjiang.

A crucial factor in the development of complex-patterned brocades was the invention of the *hua ji*, the two-storey drawloom, at the end of the 2nd century AD. This permitted a huge expansion of brocade production and also the creation of new forms such as satin and gauze ornamented with patterns in gold thread.

In ancient times the different regions of China produced different kinds of brocade such as *Song, Shu, Yun* and *Zhuang* brocades. *Shu* is a brocade that has been woven in Sichuan for 1,000 years. Its beautiful pattern is praised in the *fu* (rhyming prose) "Beautiful Woman Washing Brocade in the Shu River on a Spring Day": "The fragrant trees reflect in the mountain stream, The rosy clouds shine to the depths of the lake." "Cloud" brocade was another highly prized form with the colour of clouds. It was first produced in the 5th and 6th centuries AD, during the period of the Northern and

Impressions of silk wrappings long since rotted away mark an axe blade more than 3,000 years old. The axe was placed in a tomb in Anyang. The texture of the silk wrappings which once covered it has left a pattern of weaving in the patina which now corrodes the blade. Silk was also used to wrap bodies preserved by chemicals.

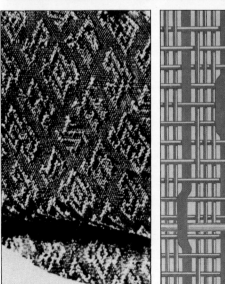

A 2,000-year-old silk workshop carved onto a stone slab in the later Han dynasty (25–220 AD). At the left of the shop, a man works a loom with foot treadles. To his right, a woman turns a wheel that reels the silk. This scene was carved at the time of the opening of the "Silk Road" between Rome and China, when silk was a Chinese monopoly.

(Left) This early piece of silk was placed in a tomb 2,200 years ago. The raised design was created by the use of pattern rods which lift the warp in a predetermined sequence.

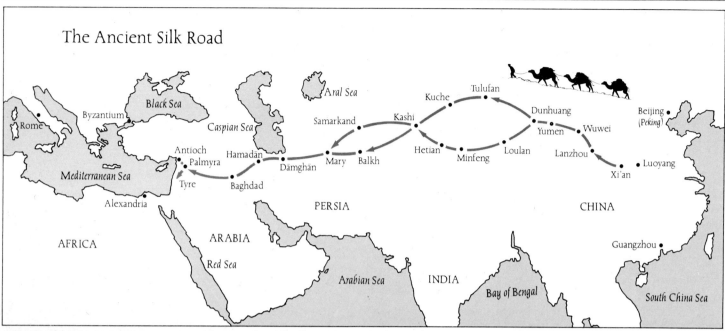

The Ancient Silk Road

Silkworms, the caterpillars of the silk moth, feed only on mulberry leaves. After mating, the female lays her eggs which hatch into tiny larvae. They eat voraciously, growing 30 times

in length and up to 10,000 times in weight. After about 30 days, the larva stops growing and, by secreting liquid silk which solidifies in air, spins a cocoon made of a single thread about 1 km long.

The old "Silk Road" stretched 8,000 km across the deserts, mountains and grasslands of Asia from Byzantium, the eastern capital of the Roman Empire, to the capital of China. Traders led camels carrying silk, jade and lacquerware from China to return with wool, ivory and gold. Marco Polo travelled this road in 1271, as did news of the wealth and inventions of China.

Silkworms have been raised in China for about 5,000 years. They are reared in trays that are kept clean and continually covered with fresh mulberry leaves. A silk industry is only possible in a settled society that is able to free the intensive labour required at each of its stages.

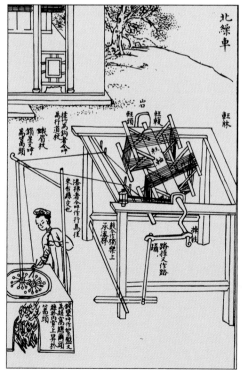

During filature silk cocoons are boiled and their threads wound on a reeling machine turned by a crank foot treadle. The silk industry's need for technology such as this encouraged China's early lead in mechanical engineering.

Southern Dynasties when China was again divided into a number of conflicting kingdoms.

China's early mastery and monopoly of sericulture led to her first important trading contacts with the west. In 138 BC, during the third year of the reign of the great Emperor Wu of the Former Han dynasty, the envoy Zhang Qian was dispatched to the western border regions. His successful diplomacy cleared the way for the establishment of the "Silk Road" between China and the shores of the Mediterranean. Direct contact between China and Rome was not made and the two great empires, then at the peak of their powers, continued to have only the vaguest comprehension of each other's customs. But a flourishing trade did develop and along with the silk of China came many of her ideas and inventions that were to have a profound impact on the history of the western world.

Silk remains as one of the foundations of China's trade, industry and culture, with continual progress being made in the technology that now makes it available to people everywhere.

Brocade is woven from coloured silk, often with gold and silver thread, in raised patterns of great richness. It has been made in China for 3,100 years where its status and value are expressed in the name *jin bo,* meaning "gold-silk."

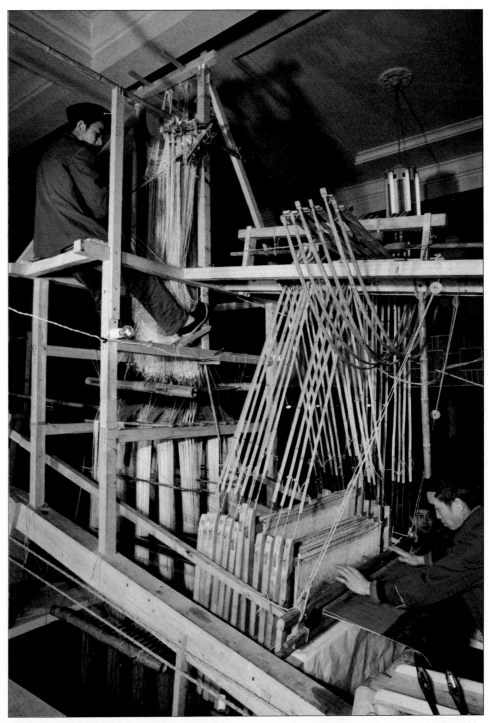

The drawloom, invented in the 2nd century AD, is used for weaving brocade. The weaver has the warp threads stretching out before him; the drawboy sits above them. As the weaver throws the weft thread between the warps, the drawboy pulls on cords tied to different sets of warp threads according to a predetermined sequence which forms the raised pattern on the brocade.

By enabling the Chinese to produce elaborate brocade quickly, the drawloom compensated for the smuggling of the secret of silk production to the west in the 6th century AD. The drawloom reached the west in the 14th century and was in common use until Jacquard's 18th century loom replaced the drawboy with a chain of punched cards.

Silk Embroidery

The history of embroidery in China is as long as the history of silk. According to the *Book of History* the Emperor Shun who reigned more than 4,200 years ago had embroidered on his robes the "Twelve Ornaments": the sun, moon, stars, mountain, dragon, pheasant, temple goblet, pondweed, flames, grains of rice, hatchet and the *fu* or "symbol of distinction." Only the emperor was permitted to wear all of these designs.

Archaeological evidence for embroidery dates back to the Western Zhou period, 11th-8th centuries BC. In 1974 the tomb of a concubine was excavated in Bao Ji, Shaanxi province and in it were found impressions of strands of plaited stitch embroidery. During the Han dynasty, which began in 206 BC, embroidery techniques developed and the art became widespread. According to the scientific and philosophical *Treatise on Salt and Iron* of Huan Kuan, the rich people of that time wore elaborately embroidered silk clothes, hung their homes and tombs with embroidered curtains and gave silk shoes to their concubines and maidservants, while their dogs and horses wore embroidered trappings.

During the Song dynasty (960-1279 AD) embroidery gradually developed from decoration for clothes into an art form specializing in the imitation of paintings and the calligraphy of famous artists. A typical example is the picture "Travelling Past the Jade Terrace on a Crane's Back" embroidered on a round fan with the aid of hair-thin needles. Using stitches that seem to fly in all directions, the artist has managed to capture the energy of the original painting in all its vigour.

Chinese embroidery began as a people's art. The traditional styles are rich in symbols of the beauty of life and of love of life. The embroidery "Mandarin Ducks on a Lotus Pond" depicts a pair of mandarin ducks–symbols of fidelity and love–playing in an idyllic patch of water lit by the sun but shaded by willow trees. A pillow and a perfume pouch are embroidered with a box, a fingered citron and plum blossoms–symbolic of peaceful years in succession, numerous children and infinite happiness.

In the past, especially talented folk embroiderers were often sent to work at the Imperial Palace. An example of their work is the "One Hundred Boys" jacket embroidered for the empress of the Ming Emperor Wan Li. Embroidered on it are numerous dragons, the character *shou* (meaning "long life") and 100 boys catching birds, playing hide-and-seek, flying kites and pretending to be officials by wearing black gauze caps.

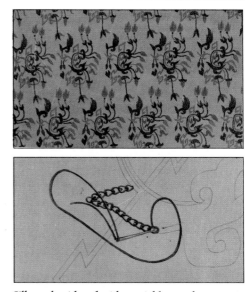

Silk, embroidered with a prickly peach pattern, found in the tomb of a Han noblewoman of the Han dynasty shows the quality of embroidery 2,200 years ago. The design was executed in fine chainstitch. Peaches have always been a popular theme, representative of longevity.

The "100 Boys" jacket of Empress Xiao Jing is embroidered in gold, silver and coloured silk with figures of dragons, bamboo, flowers and 100 boys playing games, flying kites, catching birds and pretending to be officials. All are symbols of good luck, long life and fertility. Xiao Jing was a consort of the Wan Li emperor, 1573–1619, a contemporary of Elizabeth I.

Around the edge of the jacket, embroidered in gold thread, are the "Eight Treasures": pine trees, bamboo, plum blossom, rocks and all kinds of flowers and plants.

Chinese embroidery styles are highly regionalized with the most famous examples coming from Suzhou, Hunan, Guangdong and Sichuan. *Suzhou embroidery* reflects the wealth in the artistic essentials of "opportunity, environment, material, craftsmen," which are to be found in abundance in this beautiful city set beside Taihu lake, surrounded by green hills and watered by clear streams. Reflecting their inheritance of the tradition of embroidered pictures of the Song dynasty of 1,000 years ago, the Suzhou embroiderers create "brush strokes" with fine thread and dense, smooth stitches.

A development of this technique is double-sided embroidery. Using a silk base as thin as a cicada's wing, the embroiderer may use thread only one-forty-eighth as thick as normal and a variety of stitches to represent detail as delicate as the fine structure of the tail of a goldfish. Thousands of knots and ends of thread are skilfully concealed so that the finished work is perfect when viewed from either side. In the description of the *Private Collections* compiled by Zhang Yingwen during the Ming dynasty (1368-1644), he said of Suzhou embroidery that "The mountains and streams may be enjoyed either as distant shades or as close objects. The buildings stand in three dimensions. The figures are lifelike with vivid expressions, the flowers and birds are depicted in different shapes and colours."

Hunan embroidery also melds the skills of painting and needlework. Different kinds of stitches are used to imitate different brush-styles in gold thread and more than 700 colours. An example is the huge screen "Adding Flowers to the Brocade" in which there is a peacock so lifelike it could almost come out of the screen at one's call.

Guangdong embroidery is characterized by its stylistic cohesiveness in spite of its wide range of subjects, bright colours and rich designs. "Waiting for the Moonrise at the Western Chamber" is based on the tale of Cui Yingying and Zhang Shen (the Chinese "Romeo and Juliet") told in the play the *Romance of the Western Chamber.* It is a tale of two young lovers who try to break the fetters of feudal society in their fight for the freedom to marry one another. In this embroidered picture Cui Yingying is shown standing by the garden gate, quietly waiting for Zhang Sheng. Her eyes measure less than half a centimetre, yet they are embroidered with dozens of threads of different colours which give them lifelike brilliance.

Sichuan embroidery is produced in and around the city of Chengdu, capital of Sichuan province. Its stitches are neat, the threads shiny, tight and soft. In the embroidery "Bamboo and Carp" open stitches are used to depict the delicacy and translucency of the fins while thick and thin stitches are used to reproduce the structure of the scales. The water is left quite unrepresented and yet the carp seem to be swimming.

Today the art of embroidery continues to develop. There are 50 different stitches and thousands of ways of combining threads of different colours. Reproducing the delicate brush-strokes of water-colour painting, the artist in silk can draw with strength or extreme delicacy the mountain villages, rare flowers and birds of the motherland.

A woman from Hunan province works on a piece of double-sided embroidery. It is so fine she may use single threads of silk and needles slimmer than hair. A piece this size may take hundreds of hours to finish and be worth thousands of dollars. Every loose end will be snipped off with scissors–another Chinese invention–and tucked away to leave both sides equally smooth and perfect.

This double-sided embroidery of goldfish mounted in a rosewood frame is so delicate it may be placed in a shaft of sunlight and viewed as a transparency. Goldfish, bred as pets and as food for thousands of years, are a popular theme, symbolic of vigour and great longevity. Children are often told that goldfish turn into dragons by leaping out of the water.

Architecture

The earliest architectural remains found in China date back 7,000 years, the age of Hemudu village, excavated in Zhejiang province in 1973. In 1954 archaeologists had found a village at Banpo in Shansi province, 5,000 years old. Even at this time, the late prehistoric period, the houses had wooden frames held together by mortise and tenon joints.

Three thousand years later, when China was a slave-owning society, the development of techniques for making high, thick walls of pounded earth led to the building of palaces, tombs and gardens on a grand scale. By the late 5th century BC China was entering her feudal age and the arts of building were becoming a sophisticated technology. During the Qin and Han dynasties of the 3rd and 2nd centuries BC the traditional forms of Chinese architecture began to emerge: wooden towers with stone foundations, brick walls and tiled roofs supported by systems of corbel bracketing.

Between the 5th and 10th centuries AD the coming of Buddhism brought many great innovations: cave temples with huge carved statues and wall paintings and the first pagodas. Architecture at this time tended to be massive and sturdy. During the Song dynasty of the 10th–13th centuries it became more elegant and refined. These developments were greatly influenced and standardized by the book *Ying Zao Fa Shi (Architectural Methods)* of the architect and master builder Li Jie which included a complete synopsis of the traditional techniques of Chinese architecture. These reached their final maturity in the period after the 14th century during the Ming and Qing dynasties. By this time the basic architectural forms were well established: city walls, dwellings of brick and tile, the layout of cities, palaces and parks.

Chinese Building Techniques: The Wooden Framework

"Even if the walls fall down, the house will not collapse." This proverb emphasizes vividly the fundamental principles of Chinese architecture. The wall serves only as a curtain that fills in spaces. A traditional building is supported by its wooden frame. Massive cedar pillars were erected on stone plinths resting on pounded earth founda-

(Above) This 7,000-year-old piece of timber once formed the tenon part of a mortise and tenon joint in an old ferry building. It was excavated from a neolithic site in south China (left) covering an area of 40,000 square metres. Many wooden objects have been excavated from this site, providing important archaeological data on Chinese architecture.

A 17th century architectural drawing illustrates the constructional features of Chinese buildings. Rows of massive cedar posts are connected by tiers of heavy crossbeams. Each tier is narrower than the tier below to give the heavy tiled roof its characteristic concave form. By distributing the force throughout the structure, this design is earthquake-resistant.

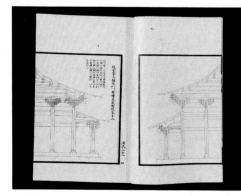

The *Architectural Methods* of Li Jie, 1103 AD, written on orders from the emperor, established building standards that lasted in China until recent times. The 1,078 wood-block-printed pages contain lists of materials, dimensions, approved costs and plans for eight grades of public buildings. Li Jie's sources dated back to the Han dynasty 1,000 years earlier. This work is a major reason that Chinese architecture changed only slightly through 2,000 years which saw all kinds of building experiments in the west.

tions around the building's perimeter. The pillars were tied together by sills at their bases and lintels at the top. Crowning the columns were nests of corbel brackets. These served to shorten the free span of the cross-beams and provided anchorage for the bracket arms which supported the characteristically wide, overhanging eaves. The cross-beams were laid one upon the other in several tiers, each one narrower than the last to give the roof its concave slope. In low roofs the beams were separated by thick blocks of wood but in high roofs they were separated by queen posts, culminating in the central ridgepole or king post. Longitudinal timbers called purlins were laid along the tops of the ridgepoles and the ends of the cross-beams to support the massive tiled roof. The wooden frame did not contain a single nail. All the timbers were joined by mortises and tenons, several thousand in a single building. Held firm by the great weight of the roof the frame was at once highly elegant and extremely flexible, equally suited to China's hot summers and snowy winters and able to withstand high winds and earthquakes.

The Layout of Chinese Buildings

For more than 2,000 years the basic form in Chinese architecture has been the courtyard enclosed by three or four buildings. The buildings face into the courtyard and form a symmetrical balance about the central axis. The buildings may be built into the wall that surrounds the courtyard or the wall may be quite separate, forming an outer corridor around the entire structure. This layout was fundamental to the dwelling places of peasants and emperors alike. In a palace the buildings were much larger and far more luxurious and the courtyards were repeated to form a succession along the north-south axis. The best known example of this is the Imperial Palace in Beijing.

In 1407 AD the Ming emperor Cheng Zu gathered more than 200,000 artisans and labourers from all over China who spent 14 years completing the palace complex. The entire "Purple Forbidden City" occupies 720,000 square metres and contains nearly 10,000 rooms. A series of huge gates flanked by stone lions, corridors, arched bridges and monuments are arranged to draw the visitor in to the centre of the palace which is

Nests of corbel brackets topping cedar columns support the massive overhanging roof of a Chinese building. The columns are held in place by lintels and cross-beams. Corbel brackets bear the roof through myriad joints which absorb earth tremors so a building may shake but not fall down. Bracket arms project out of the brackets to support the eaves. The roof consists of long purlins covered with heavy tiles. Walls are non-structural—mere partitions.

An architect's model shows how corbel brackets fit together. Standards of carpentry were high, for a building might contain thousands of joints but no nails. Chinese buildings compared very favourably with the rough Viking halls and Tudor half-timber houses that were their contemporaries.

divided into a public front area and a private rear area. In the former, with its Tai He, Zhong He and Bao He halls the emperors conducted their important ceremonies and met court officials.

The emperors lived in the domestic quarters at the rear of the palace where only the empress, the imperial concubines and the court eunuchs were allowed to enter. Here there were separate palaces such as the Qian Qing for the emperor, the Kun Ning for the empress and several others for the lesser consorts and the concubines. From front to back the palace is a unified whole–an example of the "frozen music" or "painting in three dimensions" that is the essence of Chinese architecture.

The Planning of Ancient Chinese Cities

The ancient cities of China were also laid out according to a precise geometric plan. In Changan, capital of the Sui and Tang dynasties and Beijing of the Ming and Qing dynasties, the important government buildings were oriented facing north-south along the central axis of the city. At the centre were the south-facing buildings of the Imperial Palace itself. The rest of the city radiated away from the major north-south and east-west intersecting avenues in a gridiron pattern bounded by the city walls with their corner bastions and great gate towers at the four cardinal points: north, south, east and west.

The Architectural Art of the Chinese Garden

As long ago as the 14th century BC, slaves were employed in the building of parks for their feudal masters. These parks evolved into perfect miniature landscapes complete with transplanted trees, birds and animals and winding waterways. Dotted about the parks were pavilions, terraces, corridors and arbours. Some of the emperors had summer palaces where, instead of buildings being laid out on a rigid geometric plan that mirrored the planning of the city, they were sited to harmonize with and complement the landscape. This can be seen today in the Summer Palace just to the north of Beijing.

The Summer Palace is built on the south slope of Wan Shou hill and along the north shore of Kunming lake. A long, covered

The Qi Nian hall of the Temple of Heaven, south of the palace: massive cedar posts topped by corbel brackets support a three-tiered, blue-glazed tile roof 30 m wide and 38 m high. This was the site of the annual sacrifice to Heaven which ensured security for the empire and a rich harvest. These sacrifices were last made in 1915.

The Imperial Palace, Beijing, built in 1407 AD, is a series of south-facing audience halls which front on broad courtyards. The area behind is far more intimate: gardens and small private palaces for the emperor, his empress and his concubines. The "Forbidden City" covers 720 000 m² within massive walls surrounded by a moat. More than 200,000 artisans and labourers took 14 years to complete it.

walkway and stone balustrades wind down the hill and encircle the lake as far as the approaches of a beautiful 17-arch bridge which crosses to an artificial island in the middle of the lake. The kilometre-long corridor which forms an enclosed walkway along the northern shore of the lake was used by the emperors and empresses as they took their exercise.

Chinese gardens were carefully planned to seem natural–wild and full of surprises, just like real landscapes. They were to seem as though "Heaven itself had made them", complete with flowering trees, waterfalls and pinnacles of grotesquely shaped limestone. Gardens had enormous significance for the Chinese. They were places of retreat with their own pavilions where a person could live to draw, paint, philosophize or write poetry.

Chinese Civil Engineering

From the dawn of civilization to the present, two great preoccupations have shaped the expertise of China's civil engineers: the need to control the waters of her rivers, with their capricious tendency to both flood and drought, and to defend the nation against the enemies of the Chinese people who live to the north. The diversion and irrigation scheme at Guan county on the Min River in Sichuan province is as effective now as it was 2,200 years ago when, as reported by the great historian Sima Qian: "Li Bing the governor cut through the shoulder of a mountain to make the 'Separated Hill' and abolished the ravages of the Min River, excavating the two great canals in the plain of Chengdu."

What Li Bing did was to divert the bulk of the waters of the Min River (leaving enough for boat transport) into an irrigation system that served an area of 60 x 75 km which now supports a population of more than five million people. The most difficult part of this operation was the cutting of the "Cornucopia Channel" (Bao Ping Kou) 30 m wide and 40 m deep. This feeds a total of 526 lateral and 2,200 sub-lateral canals in the Chengdu plain, supplying water which not only provides irrigation and freedom from flood or drought but drives (according to a stone tablet erected in the Yuan period 650 years ago) "water wheels for hulling and grinding rice and for spinning and weaving machinery to the number of tens

Entered through a "Moon Gate" and adorned with pools, bridges and pavillions, Chinese gardens have been favourite retreats for poets, philosophers and lovers for more than 3,000 years. Particularly famous are the gardens of the city of Suzhou. Here, careful shaping of the land and the planting of trees, bamboos and grotesque limestone rocks serve to re-create the rugged, mysterious geography of south China. Flowers were less important in these gardens although China gave the west peonies, camellias, roses and azaleas.

A rubbing of a map of Ping Jiang, today's Suzhou, carved on a stone slab 800 years ago, depicts the "gridiron" layout characteristic of most Chinese cities. The grand buildings face south, with the most important at the centre. Streets run north-south, east-west. The broadest avenues along the main axes connect the city gates. These pierce a massive wall of pounded earth and rubble which is enclosed by a moat.

of thousands operating throughout the four seasons."

Li Bing's waterworks were completed in 230 BC in the state of Shu which had been conquered in 316 BC by the state of Qin. In 221 BC Qin succeeded in conquering the last of the Warring States, thus unifying China. One of its great generals, Meng Tian was sent with 300,000 men to drive off the barbarians who had invaded the northern frontier regions and make their return impossible by building China's most famous monument and the world's largest man-made structure–the Great Wall.

Defensive walls had been built by some of the Warring States as early as the 5th century BC. These were linked up and extended to make the *Wan Li Chang Cheng* ("Long Wall of Ten Thousand Li") which is actually more than 12,700 *li* (6,350 km) long. The wall we can see today is the reconstruction built during the Ming dynasty about 500 years ago. Like a great dragon, it flies from west to east, straddling deserts, grasslands and mountain ranges to the sea.

With their numerous and often difficult rivers the Chinese were forced to become the world's leading bridge builders. An early invention was the suspension bridge, the longest of which is the Zhu Pu bridge across the Min River, Sichuan, just above Li Bing's famous divide and cut in Guan county. It has eight spans totalling 350 m in length supported by ten bamboo cables 10-12 cm in diameter. Bamboo is an ideal building material for structures such as these; nevertheless, it was replaced by iron in some instances as early as 1,400 years

The Anji bridge across the Xiao river is nearly 1,400 years old although it looks like it was built yesterday. It is the world's first segmental arch bridge, a low curve of masonry firmly wedged between the river banks with relief arches to allow flood water to escape.

A building site is prepared on a site aligned north-south, with the entrance to the south. Men pound the earth with doughnut-shaped stones and hollow logs with handles while others scrape off high spots, fill in low spots and lay the stones which will support the columns.

ago–1,200 years before the first chain-link suspension bridge was built in Europe.

The Chinese were also superb builders of stone bridges and the Anji bridge built across the Xiao River in Hebei province is perhaps the most outstanding example. Erected under the mason Li Chun between 605-617 AD the Anji or "Peaceful Crossing" arch bridge is nearly 51 m long with a single span of nearly 38 m and a height of only 7.25 m. This is the world's first segmental arch bridge with a mainspan in the form of a segment of an arch rather than a full half circle. This makes it lighter, stronger and lower than full-arch bridges – the latter making it much easier for road traffic to cross. The shoulders of the bridge are pierced twice, reducing the amount of masonry in the bridge and hence its weight, and also allowing water to pass through at time of floods, water that might otherwise have swept the bridge away. The effectiveness of the design and construction of the Anji bridge is proven by the fact of its having stood, regardless of floods and earthquakes, for more than 1,300 years, as well as its having been imitated the world over since the 14th century – when it was already 800 years old.

Three hundred thousand labourers worked from 221-214 BC to join and extend many smaller walls into the Great Wall. The wall is as wide as two chariots on top, 6,350 km long, 10 m high, and has towers every 30-40 m. It was built to keep out the nomadic raiders to the north-west who, in time of peace, came to sell their splendid horses to the Chinese.

Traditional Handicrafts

Huge areas of south China are covered with forests of bamboo. More than 2,200 years ago bamboo weaving was practised during the Zhou dynasty. In Sichuan there is an ancient proverb: "Wang Qiao Shou ('Skillful Wang') was a clever craftsman who made things from strips of bamboo, even birds that could fly and human figures that could speak. When the emperor heard of this he sent men to arrest Wang. But when he heard they were coming, Wang wove the Wu mountain and the Qin mountain out of bamboo in one night and thus prevented the emperor doing violence to him."

Bamboo has natural colours of light green and pale yellow. It is tough, flexible and possesses enormous tensile strength. Bamboo may be split as thin as wires and woven into bags, baskets, vases, plates, hats, farm tools, etc., all exquisite and with a distinct local flavour. In summer, while chatting in the moonlight, the cunning bamboo workers may produce toys at random. In less than five minutes they can weave a frog from just three bamboo strips—a frog with a spring inside that hops at the press of a finger! In recent decades the variety of colours and designs possible has been enormously increased with the introduction of red, black and blue paints. Other plant materials used in weaving are palm fibre, cattail stems, wheat straw, rattan and twigs of the chaste tree.

Kites were called "woodhawk" or "windhawk" in ancient times. The first record, "whittling bamboo to make a crow, then flying it," dates back more than 2,000 years. In the 3rd century BC, Gong Shuban made a "woodhawk" to spy upon the Song city. In the 2nd century BC Zhang Liang flew a "hawk" with a man on it who played a vertical flute to sap the morale of the Chu troops. These are the first records of the use of kites in war but in time of peace they were and still are a source of endless fun for the people both as plaything and as serious sport. Kites were originally made of bamboo or wood but later they were made of paper or silk. Kites in south China are different from those of the north. In the south the

Bamboo praying mantis

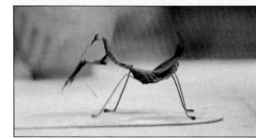

(Left) Two cups and a basket made of bamboo. Sliced into slivers of great tensile strength (below) bamboo is woven into baskets, hats and toys. There are nearly 1,000 species of this versatile grass, some delicate, others as thick as a man's arm and 40 m tall. Bamboo is indispensable to Chinese civilization. Needles, knives, rope-bridges, gun-barrels, rockets, fire crackers, umbrella spokes, fishing rods, the apparatus of the alchemists—all have been made of bamboo.

Fans carried by women, workmen and soldiers alike are essential in China's hot, sultry summer climate. They are usually made of strips of bamboo covered with paper or silk or adorned with paintings of flowers, landscapes or characters from legends, accompanied by elegant poems. Others are of palm leaves or delicate strips of ivory. Among the most beautiful are the scented sandalwood fans of Suzhou, cut with a fretsaw and highlighted with the touch of a hot poker.

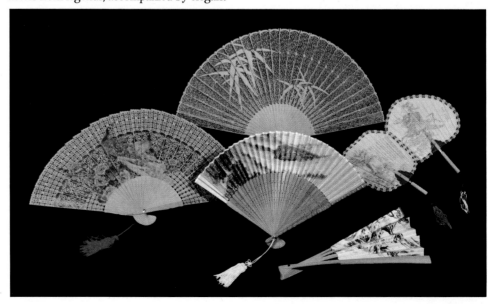

winds are usually light so most kites have soft wings and are shaped like dragonflies, butterflies, phoenixes, cranes, etc. In the north the wind is strong and so are the wings of the kites which may be shaped like swallows, goldfish, classical figures–the designs are too numerous to be counted!

Chinese papercutting is a delicate folk art with a history of at least 1,000 years. In its praise the famous modern poet Guo Moruo wrote: "This superb craftsmanship with scissors excels the work of the Creator and leaves eternal beauty among the people." The art of Chinese papercutting can be summarized in five words: pointed, round, thin, square, notched. It can be "as pointed as an awn of wheat," "as round as an autumn moon or a bright mirror," "as fine and wavy as the long beard of an old man," "as square as the corners of a newly made brick" and "notched like the teeth of a saw or the crenellations of the top of a wall." Chinese papercuts are popular everywhere–flowers for window decorations in the northern countryside, embroidered shoe designs in mid-China, the appliqué of Guangdong.

The most famous clay sculptures are made in Hui Shan near the city of Wuxi in Jiangsu province. They may be crude articles for peasants and children which usually represent things in everyday life and are symbols of good luck and happiness. At spring ploughing time peasants often buy a clay buffalo and present it to their relatives or friends, saying, "Just touch the buffalo's head and you won't worry about your food," thus wishing them a bountiful harvest in the following summer. Some people will buy a *Da Ah Fu* ("Big Happy Baby") in the hope that their children will be healthy and safe from accidents. The making of these articles is very simple and they can be completed at a single sitting. The chief concern is to give lively expression to the faces and only bright colours such as red, green, gold, white and pink are used.

The more refined clay sculptures are chiefly characters from the traditional operas. These colourful sculptures are shaped out of sticky, smooth, porcelain clay then painted with water colours. Working up a sculpture includes more than a dozen stages including clay-pounding, sketching, shaping, making moulds, casting, stamping, polishing, whitewashing, colouring, drawing on the features and varnishing. The

Large, delicate kites like this dragon are made for the light winds of south China. Those made in the north are simpler and more rugged. The earliest record of a kite dates from the 3rd century BC when a general of one of the Warring States used a "woodhawk" to spy on the enemy. This was 1,800 years before the west learned how to make kites from the Chinese and took the first step toward the invention of the airplane. Kite flying remains a popular sport across China to this day.

Folk artists have cut paper patterns almost since paper was invented. (Above right) A tower surrounded by a "dragon wall" and (right) two mandarin ducks paddling between lotus leaves–symbolic of married bliss amidst fruitfulness.

Miniature clay sculptures are a popular adjunct to the art of Chinese ceramics. Favourite subjects include characters from old folk tales and operas, like the popular and mischievous "Monkey King" seen here with the monk Tripitaka and the reformed ruffians "Pigsy" and "Sandy." According to the tale, these four made the "Journey to the West" on the emperor's orders– a quest that brought the Buddhist scriptures to China 1,500 years ago.

style is bold and romantic with lifelike facial expressions.

In China, fans are not merely summer comforts but works of art. Suzhou fans are made of silk, paper and feathers. Feather fans are woven of goose or crane feathers and may be rectangular or circular in shape. Their handles are made of mottled bamboo, bone, ivory or red sandalwood. Silk fans are made of thin, tough silk pasted onto bamboo frames of various shapes: hexagonal, octagonal, gourd-shaped, round. Their handles are carved into the S-shape of a *ruyi*–symbol of good luck–and tassels are attached to them. Silk fans are painted with traditional designs in fine, close, detailed brushwork or in freehand–figures, landscapes, flowers, birds, insects, fish; brightly coloured or misty and elegant. Folding fans have nine to thirty ribs pinned together with thick ribs at the ends. They may be made of "freckled green," "water ground" or "plum concubine" bamboo, *nanmu* or red or white sandalwood, ivory, horn or turtle shell. The fan is covered with soft cotton paper, tigerskin paper striped with gold, gold-freckled paper, etc. Folded fans often contain miniature masterpieces of calligraphy and painting. They may also be made of thin palm or cattail leaves, bamboo or wood strips.

The Chinese carve in jade, wood, lacquer and ivory as well as stone, which has been carved since prehistoric times when early men made stone tools. Massive stone carving began in the Han dynasty in the 2nd and 3rd centuries BC. An early example is the statue of the famous irrigation engineer, Li Bing, more than 2 m high. Later, many figures appeared such as those in the Yun Gang and Long Men Buddhist grottoes. The stone Buddhas in these caves are up to 17 m high, carved with superb skill and full of life. In the Long Men grottoes there are nearly 100,000 of these figures. More common than this kind of carving is the use of stone as an indispensable part of traditional Chinese architecture –ornamental columns *(hua biao)*, carved balustrades, stone tablets and small but exquisite details. Since the 14th century AD Shoushan stone has often been used for sculpture in China. The artist first examines his stone, then he chooses his subject and lays out the design according to the shape, arrangement of veins and colour of the

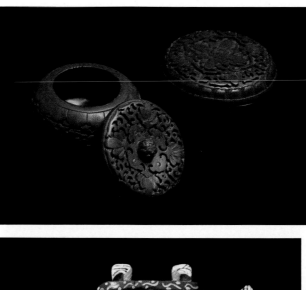

Painted wooden masks were worn during the Lantern Festival, held in the second month to celebrate the coming of Spring. In the head-dress of this mask a tiger peers out beneath a pair of dragons who are about to devour a pearl (symbolic of the moon) while two more dragons flank it with their tails.

The red lacquer which covers these pots is made from the sap of the lac tree. It is gathered like maple syrup and thickened over a slow fire. Cinnabar (red mercuric sulphide) gives it its vermillion colour. Black lacquer is darkened with soot. The pots were dipped in the lacquer many times (40 is common, 200 possible) to create a thick layer that can be carved. Lacquer was exported along the "Silk Road" and while legend has it that it was made 4,400 years ago, the oldest pieces extant are 2,500 years old.

Furniture is often coated with black lacquer, providing a perfect surface for painting, sometimes with gold.

Jade can't be marked by any metal; it can only be worked with soft copper cutting wheels impregnated with fine abrasive mud made from crushed garnet, emery, ruby or quartz. A piece like this may take a year to finish. The beauty and hardness of jade make it almost sacred, a symbol of the "Five Virtues": charity, equity, wisdom, courage and rectitude.

stone. Then he sketches on the design with a brush and begins to carve a crude outline, taking care as he does so to conceal any defects in the stone while making the most of its beauty. When the outline is roughed out he carves the details and finally waxes and polishes the sculpture to finish a superb piece of art.

A Miao woman from south-west China uses molten wax to block areas of cloth from taking her indigo dye. The technique of pattern dyeing, called "batik," is known throughout south-east Asia.

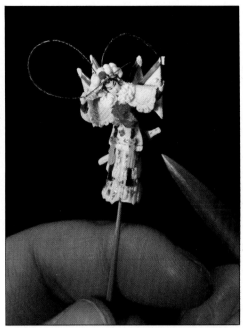

Mu Guei Ying, the "Woman Warrior"–a popular Chinese heroine, is fashioned out of coloured dough with tiny knives and the points of needles. Flour dough is mixed with watercolour pigments before it is shaped into these exquisite figurines. When they are finished, the dough models are simply left to dry in the sun.

This magnificent lantern is of rosewood with tassels of silk and thin panes of translucent gauze. Inside is a fan with whirling figures turned by the heat of the lamp. Lanterns may also be simple, of bamboo and thin paper. No festival is complete without them.

The *sheng* is a reed organ. Its 17 pipes are of 5 lengths with reeds at their lower ends. They fit into a lacquered wind chest which has a mouthpiece and a metal slider. Music played an important part in ancient ritual and was considered essential to the education of all people.

There are eight classes of Chinese musical instruments: stone (chimes), metal (bells), bamboo (pan pipes), silk (lutes), wood ("tiger boxes"), gourd ("shengs"), skin (drums), and earthenware (ocarinas). Chinese music is highly mathematical but it also has mystic associations. These date back 4,200 years to the legendary emperor Shun who "tuned the pitchpipes", which were used in divination.

Miniature dough modelling is not an ancient craft. It has been practised for about 100 years. Once a means for peasants to obtain a little pocket money, it has since become a fine art. Popular subjects are scenes from ancient legends that may be placed in "landscapes" made of cork or stone and characters from the opera and novels that may be so small they fit into walnut shells.

Rivers of Science

Joseph Needham
Director, East Asian History of Science Library, Cambridge University. Joseph Needham is the world's pre-eminent authority on Chinese science and author of definitive books on the subject.

When, forty years ago, we began our work on the systematic history of science, technology and medicine in China, things were very different from what they are like today. China was only just beginning to acquire the status of a world power, and people everywhere were only just beginning to show that intense curiosity about all things Chinese which has been so strongly manifested in the subsequent years. The professional sinologists told us that there was nothing to be gained by such studies as we intended to pursue; China, they said, was and had always been a land of peasant-farmers and a few scholar-poets running a government of "imperial oriental despotism." It did not take us very long to appreciate the complete falsity of this attitude.

Many people often realise some of the great things that were done in China in ancient and medieval times, but after that they talk of a "stagnation" which overcame Chinese culture. We do not believe in this at all; what we say is that the course of discovery and invention in China went on slowly all through the ages, but was finally altogether overtaken by the rise of *modern* science since the beginning of the seventeenth century. The Greeks probably reached heights which the Chinese never did, but on the other hand the Chinese had nothing corresponding to the Dark Ages–which really were dark as far as science and technology were concerned. In order to have a proper historical perspective one must have a clear idea of what constitutes modern science (as opposed to ancient and medieval science) and we say that its essence lies in the mathematization, and if possible the quantization, of hypotheses about Nature, these being then tested by persistent experimentation. But modern science was not the only sort of science. Science had been growing up throughout the ancient and medieval times in all civilisations. All of them had their great achievements, and the knowledge gained by the science of the ancients and the people of the Middle Ages all flowed into modern science like rivers flow to the sea.

Actually the mainsprings of our own endeavour arose from the question starkly presenting itself when younger Chinese colleagues came to work for their doctorates in Cambridge in 1937–why had modern science developed in Europe alone? It happened in the time of Galileo, the great astronomer. Leonardo da Vinci, though a genius, did not belong to the time of modern science. One might say also that Tycho Brahe did not, though Kepler perhaps did. In any case, we found soon enough that there was a second question hiding behind this first one, namely why had China been more effective for the previous fourteen centuries in acquiring knowledge of Nature and using it for human benefit than the Europeans? This is the sort of problem which will be raised in the minds of thinking people who visit this exhibition.

In approaching these problems there are, as we see it, two different viewpoints. On the one hand you can place a very great influence on all kinds of intellectual factors, on the presence or absence of monotheism, on attitudes to time and change, on language, and on the worldview in general of people in different civilisations. On the other hand, you can also place great emphasis on the social and economic factors. And it is indeed true that feudalism in China was fundamentally different from that in Europe. We would never want to undervalue the intellectual factors, but we doubt whether they will ever be sufficient by themselves to explain the whole course of the phenomenon.

It remains a fact, however unpalatable, that the rise of modern science in the West was part of the process which included the rise of capitalism and the Protestant Reformation. None of these phenomena happened in China at all, and one therefore cannot help wondering whether there was not some intimate connection between them. It seems that the rising merchants of the European city-states were able to do what the bureaucrats of the Confucian party never could do, namely bring together the intellectual disciplines of mathematics and the study of Nature. This is something to be pondered on. But equally worthy of consideration is the favourable role of the Confucian bureaucracy in earlier centuries; indeed one may say that the bureaucratic feudalism of China began by being extremely favourable to scientific development and ended by inhibiting it. No doubt as we go further on, we shall learn more–*qui vivra verra!* But at any rate, these thoughts are worthy of being pondered by those who visit this exhibition.

May I end, as I began, by wishing it every possible success, and hoping that it may be seen in many cities on both sides of the Atlantic as time goes by.